SLAM YOUR POETRY

MILES MERRILL is a performing writer who appears at festivals and events worldwide. He is the founder of Australian Poetry Slam, an international performing writers' program, which sees up to 1000 writers performing in over 80 events across the Asia-Pacific every year. Miles has hosted an ABC TV special on poetry slams, performed solo at the Sydney Opera House and published award-winning poetry in print, audio and video. As creative director of the literary arts organisation Word Travels, he focuses on empowering people from diverse and marginalised communities to share their stories and poems with the world.

NARCISA NOZICA is an English teacher with over ten years' experience. She graduated from the University of Sydney with bachelor's degrees in arts and education. In 2016, she won a NSW Premier's English Teachers Association Scholarship to study how spoken word poetry can be used in schools. Since then, she has written articles, presented at conferences on the subject of spoken word, and worked with teachers and students to help young people find their poetic voice.

SLAM

WRITE A REVOLUTION

YOUR

POETRY

MILES MERRILL AND NARCISA NOZICA

NEWSOUTH

A NewSouth book

Published by
NewSouth Publishing
University of New South Wales Press Ltd
University of New South Wales
Sydney NSW 2052
AUSTRALIA
newsouthpublishing.com

© Miles Merrill and Narcisa Nozica 2020
First published 2020

10 9 8 7 6 5 4 3 2 1

A catalogue record for this
book is available from the
National Library of Australia

ISBN   9781742236094 (paperback)
        9781742244778 (ebook)
        9781742249278 (epDF)

Cover design Design by Commitee
Internal design Josephine Pajor-Markus

UNSW
SYDNEY

CONTENTS

PART 2 SET UP A SLAM

PART 3 TEACH A REVOLUTION

THE TEASER ...

This is how you change the world with your story.

No props. No music. No costumes.

Just you, your words and a mic. You've got 2 minutes to make the crowd scream your name.

Listen to the distant rumble. The roar, getting closer. The cumulonimbus of people not being heard, people whose stories are not being told. The thunder-clap slam of poetry meets the electric light-flash of stage and cheering audience. This overpowering storm of ovations and raw solo manifestos – it's no rock concert. This isn't pop.

It's you. Yes: Y-O-U.

You're saying what's on your mind with immediate access to an audience.

This is poetry slam.

This ain't Poetry Classics 101

What is a poetry slam anyway?

It is not a shaking-piece-of-paper-in-hand, mumble-abstract-rhymes and look-at-the-floor-for-20-minutes poetry reading. This is a combination of theatre, writing, storytelling, stand-up, hip-hop and more, all compressed into ninja poetry. It's rousing anthems spoken by people who feel their stories must be heard. It's poems that tackle topics better than any politician or journalist can, spoken by people who live their words.

It's linked to a tradition of oral storytelling that goes back thousands of years (see box, pages 4–5). I talked about this with Maxine Beneba Clarke, award-winning author of *Foreign Soil* and *The Hate Race*, who was a key figure in Melbourne's poetry slam community for years before her books were published. Spoken word, she says, can be an outlet for people who don't normally feel heard.

'There are a lot of communities that have a more established history of oral storytelling. Their stories come from being passed down through generations. That's where, traditionally, stories have come from,' she says. 'There's a history of African griots [story-tellers] and Indigenous songlines and things like that, where people will gravitate more towards this live spoken thing. You're not saying you need to be able to script something and put it on a page in the way that a tertiary-educated editor of a particular magazine is going to instantly be able to digest.'

Spoken word 'shifts the bar', she adds, allowing anyone to tell stories on their own terms. 'It's like: here's the microphone … You get your turn. It doesn't matter who you are. Doesn't matter what level you are at or what your background is. You have your turn.'

A poetry slam is also an artifice. It's just a competition

thrown over the top of a poetry reading. It satisfies an ancient addiction to conflict. It's the emotional roller-coaster of story. We want to watch heroes rise. We feel heartbroken when they fall.

We applaud winners. We care about losers. If you are in the audience, you can say you watched poetry and you cheered. If you are on stage, you spoke a poem and the audience went wild.

In a poetry slam, writers perform their original work in front of an audience. The writers are given a time limit – usually 2 or 3 minutes. Their names are drawn out of a hat to determine which order they will perform in. They're scored by five judges who are chosen randomly from the audience. The judges hold up scores after each performance. In the Australian Poetry Slam, five judges are chosen often by throwing five chocolates into the audience or taping a message under five seats, or even having the MC spin around with their eyes closed and pointing a finger into the audience to choose each judge. Usually there is a timekeeper and a scorekeeper too.

Performing writers lose points for going over time. Scores are from 0 to 10 using decimal points to tenths of a point – like 8.7 or 9.3. The high score and the low score are dropped and the middle three are added up. This helps avoid bias. Say your mum gets chosen as a judge: 'Ten! Ten! Ten to the power of ten! That's my girl!' Or your ex-bff: 'Minus infinity.' A perfect score is 30. The writer with the highest score goes onto the next round or wins a prize.

STORIES BEFORE WRITING

Humans began using language about 200 000 years ago, yet our earliest evidence of writing is only about 5000 years old. So for thousands of years before writing was invented, stories had to be shared person to person – via the spoken word.

In Australia, for tens of thousands of years Indigenous Australians spoke, sang and danced their stories to describe landscapes, travelling routes, plant and animal life, mythological creatures, ancestral histories ... an entire civilisation with hundreds of languages, all connected through spoken and sung words, music, movement and pictographs. Imagine the whole of Australia mapped by poetry. Europeans called this complex conceptual network of oral culture the Dreamtime, Dreaming and songlines.

Poetry slams began in ancient Athens around 400 BC. The annual Dionysus festival sent lottery tickets across the city. If you got a ticket, you became a judge of the latest verse plays, joining a stadium of cheering audience members. The poet/playwright with the highest score got crowned with a laurel wreath. Their poetry lived, recited across the Greek empire.

Sophocles, Aeschylus and Euripides are the three playwrights we know best out of the thousands of festival entrants. Why? They won this 'slam' more times than any of their peers.

In other ancient societies, rhythmic hymns and narratives were recited to catch the ear and attention of an audience. Lyrical odes were handed down by reciting and memorising. Bards and troubadours were called upon to perform at rituals, athletic events and festivals. Their poems would celebrate the achievements of heroes or recall the important events of the time. Imagine a party where, instead of people standing around talking over music and looking for one more celery stick to wipe up that hummus with, there's a guy who's travelled to your backyard. He's got a lute. (Think fat guitar.) He spits rhymes about Obama's new job and the approaching cyclone in Queensland. He tells the news of the day through lyrics, poems and stories. Annually at poetry slams across the globe this scenario is re-enacted as poets travel to hundreds of stages, spreading spoken word that responds to current issues and events.

What kind of poetry is it?

I'll let you in on a secret: there is no such thing as 'slam poetry'. It's not a genre. It's an event format, a platform to attract audiences to poets. Remember you can do *anything* with words – tell a story, sing a cappella, perform a monologue or string together a bunch of sounds while doing a backflip. It's whatever you do with mouth, body and mic. Performing your writing is like stand-up comedy, but the emotional range goes further than just laughter. Your audience might cry, cheer or snap their fingers in collective appreciation. They might even pay you.

'Slam poet' is just a label for a person who has performed in a poetry slam. If poets performed with the same movements, cadence and themes all night long and onto YouTube, the spoken word art form would get dead boring and just turn into a parody of itself: like the poetry slam parody in *22 Jump Street*, or the comedic impressions of spoken word by Tom Hanks and Samuel L Jackson on Jimmy Fallon's *Tonight Show*.

While this book will help you write and prepare for poetry slams, it is also a guide to creating a one-person performance that can be adapted to a variety of lengths and situations – not just a slam competition.

What's in this book

This book is for writers who perform and performers who write. It's about using powerful techniques to get your writing to the world in whatever way you can. Poetry slams are just one tool for moving your words from your head to an audience. They are just one way to get an audience to listen and to help a community feel heard. There's much more to it than 2 or 3 minutes on stage in a competition. The *real* goal is to use the combination of writing and performance to propel your ideas.

This book is also for people who have never thought about getting their thoughts down on paper, and the many more who have never thought about standing up and speaking those words in front of other humans. This is a life skill. You need to learn how to tell your stories. I've taught this to the IT team at an international insurance company when they wanted to present without PowerPoint. And to a group of country town councillors when they wanted to talk to constituents about drought. And to thousands of young people in schools, youth centres and festivals who just want a creative outlet for their thoughts.

Writers often think of the isolated retreat at the foot of a New Zealand mountain where they'll tap out their master works. They may believe writing is the path of the introvert. As a writer in any genre, you are communicating with the public. If you do it well and publish, you will be invited to speak in person to live audiences. Get used to it. Write and get out there.

This is also for teachers who know that students and community groups will absolutely love it. Here you'll find out how to transform any room into a theatre and unearth the writer and performer in anyone – whether you're in a classroom, in a formal workshop or out in the community.

HOW POETRY SLAM GOT STARTED

The following is a dramatisation and should not be taken as verbatim reporting.

It was 1984. A construction worker in Chicago was writing poetry and wanted to find a place to read it. He went to an open mic night in a little bar called The Get Me High. Paid his five bucks. Sat and waited for his turn. He noticed that the audience were all looking into their laps like they were asleep. The writers on stage would shuffle through papers or thumb through notebooks, dribbling a soft stream of consonants into the microphone: 'Oh here it is – oh wait, no, no that's not it. Just a sec. Aha. Can everyone hear me okay?' They'd start up a poem, until: 'Oh wait. Sorry. I did that one last week ...' They would do this for 20 minutes or until the audience had left.

When Marc Smith, our poet/construction worker, made it onto the stage, he tried being loud and expressive but the people in the audience were distracted, scribbling into their notebooks. They were all preparing to take the stage with their own writing so they could 'perform' to people who were looking down into their notebooks preparing to get on stage and perform for people who were preparing to get on stage ...

There was no audience. It was nothing more than a pat-on-the-back club.

So, Marc started his own eclectic, theatrical poetry cabaret in that tiny club, where performance was as important as language. This drew a crowd.

In '86 a guy called Dave Jemillo was sitting in the audience. He ran the Green Mill Lounge in uptown Chicago, a venue with a much bigger capacity. Dave invited Marc to move his Sunday night poetry cabaret to the bigger joint. Marc decided he'd need something more than just poets performing for each other if he was gonna fill it with 150 people. So he turned it into a poetry slam competition that kicked off a literary movement still thriving today. His Uptown Poetry Slam at the Green Mill has run live every week since July 1986. The format was picked up in every city in the US and spread around the world. Some of the largest slam communities are in Munich, Paris and Rotterdam.

Michael Crane began running Australia's first poetry slam–style event, called Poetry Idol (before any popular TV show called *Idol*), in Melbourne in the early 1990s. I started running poetry slams with a group of four poets on Monday nights in Newtown, Sydney, in 1996. This rocket still soars through every capital city in Australia, and in dozens of towns.

Who we are

Slam Your Poetry is written by two people.

Miles

I'm Miles Merrill, a performing writer with over 20 years' experience getting in front of audiences – from a bunch of farmers in a marquee in outback New South Wales, to ABC TV, to international tours. I've run poetry slams in small towns and major cities, organising thousands of events, shows and workshops. I started the international Australian Poetry Slam program on a local scale in 2004, and three years later it went national. I also run spoken word festivals at the Sydney Opera House and direct the literary non-profit organisation Word Travels, based in Sydney.

You'll be reading my voice in Parts 1 and 2 of this book. These parts are a step-by-step guide to writing some new stuff and turning it into a performance. There'll be avenues that take you bounding out of slam into your own spoken word shows.

Narcisa

Hi, I'm Narcisa Nozica, and I've put together Part 3 of this book – how to bring spoken word and poetry slams into schools and communities. I'm a high school English teacher who knows the awesome potential of performance poetry in the classroom. When I was awarded a NSW Premier's Teacher Scholarship to research how to harness its power, I threw out everything I knew and started from scratch. Since then I've been working with students and teachers to give young people an empowering platform from which they can write to speak their personal truth.

Taking poetry from page to stage puts imaginative writing in pride of place. Having seen the way it can transform both the language and the lives of young people, I want to see that transformation start today, with you.

PART 1

WRITE TO SPEAK

1

THE PLAY BOOK

This a play book.
    It's like a workbook.
    Only different.
    You are invited to play with this book.
    Make notes.
    Underline.
    Stop.
    Go make something.
    Come back.
    Read more.
    Put the book down.
    Think.
    Pick it up.
    Put it down.
    Go make something – AGAIN!
    Until you have many somethings to share with the world.
    Save your thoughts from extinction.
    Write them down as well as speak them.
    Recite. Record. Write.

Why do it?

At a poetry slam, anything can happen. Think of 'Poetry SLAM' as an acronym and you get Poetry: Stories, Lyrics and Monologues.

In the slam's purest form, the poet is not allowed props, music or costumes and it must be your own writing. You lose points for going over time. This is what has drawn in audiences and inspired writers to become concise, powerful, dramatic, hilarious and honest with their words. It's made them cut straight into the hearts and heads of thousands of people, each artist armed only with words and body.

Because of the direct transfer of ideas and emotion to the audience, the poetry slam platform might help you speak up about a social issue you feel doesn't get enough air time. You might present a creative treatise on climate change, your own experience as a refugee, or an investigation of racial politics in country towns – or wherever

STRAIGHT TO THE POINT

'The point is not the points.
The point is the poetry.'

Marc Smith, poetry slam founder

WRITING THE PERSONAL

I was in my first year of university, in Chicago, my home city. After a night out, I missed the last bus home and fell asleep at the bus stop. I woke with peak-hour commuters whispering around me, 'I wonder if he's moved in.' Someone commented on the drool slipping down my cheek. Another mumbled about my smell.

That experience put the fear of homelessness into me. It's one of the moments that made me realise I needed to keep studying. As an African–American male in Chicago, in that moment I felt how important my ability to articulate my thoughts clearly, coherently and intelligently was. It would save me from feeling brushed aside, ignored, pigeonholed and stereotyped, unable to express who I was inside. I needed validation.

I stood up and, in my clearest 'educated' voice, said, 'Pardon me. Have I missed the 6:30 bus to Lincoln Park?'

I'm going to show you how personal stories like these become the raw material for creating poems. It's called catharsis – the release of strong or repressed emotions through action. Some people go for a run or crash into their mate on the footy field. A sculptor digs into clay or cuts marble. A writer enters a trance-like state that grows into a verbal unleashing of the experience and what it represents to them ... then takes the raw clay of that passionate first draft and creates a work of art.

MILES

the imagination and social change mix. You'll want to tell your audience about something that affects you personally, something that you're passionate about. You don't want to wait for a casting director, editor or curator to approve your work. You may have tried this and found, as I did, that the life experience of artistic gatekeepers doesn't always match your own cultural mosaic. The black actor gets asked to play 'Street Thug #3'. The graffiti artist paints the outside wall of the gallery. And so on.

Who will tell your stories? You have to. When no one is telling your stories, speak up.

Take control of the story

Stories use the language of persuasion. They are what advertisers use on us, tapping into our senses, imagination, curiosity and vulnerability while an actor juggles a box of branded fried chicken. We hate it, particularly when it's all message and no content: 'Buy my toothpaste. For just $1.99, make your smile whiter.'

A phone company creates an ad with an Australian Poetry Slam champion reciting a story about the magic of technology over the top of emotive imagery. Two million people watch, comment, like and share. Does is it count as poetry? Can the story stand up as powerful literature? Is advertising art? Are copywriters poets who've chosen a better pay cheque?

Most of the transfer of knowledge is done by people in control of the platforms for sharing information: news

TELEPORTING

'I definitely love the connection I get to experience with an audience. Leading them on journeys and having them there with me, knowing they're feeling my work, or that I've transported them somewhere, or even rallying them into some sort of positive social action – it all demonstrates the power of poetry.'

Candy Royalle, poet and activist

companies, TV networks, social media corporations, tech giants. What are these companies interested in? Is it money? Their product? Their founders' world view? When poetry enters the realm of corporate bottom lines, there is a risk that people will stop trusting the poem and the poet. Would you believe a poem or story that was just trying to get you to switch internet service providers?

But these formal filters for shared ideas are losing their power. Many platforms for telling stories are now accessible to you and me. We can hear directly from the independent individuals, the artists, the students, the educators and activists, the people who pick up a book called Slam Your Poetry: Write a revolution. Anyone can now share an idea and have it liked or commented on.

TELL IT LIKE IT IS

'We see so many people of colour, particularly kids of Middle Eastern and African origin, telling their stories in these amazing ways. I don't think that they necessarily would have been comfortable doing that 15 years ago without the rise of spoken word. I think it can only be a positive thing.'

Omar Musa, spoken word poet, novelist, hip-hop artist and 2008 Australian Poetry Slam Champion

Artists also embed their messages in narrative and metaphor. The stop-immigration-detention poem. The gender-identity song. The end-climate-change film. The deeper and more personal you make your story, the more emotional impact your message will have. When you show that you trust the audience thiiiis much (hands stretched wide) with your deepest feelings, they will feel you have pulled off the veil of 'stranger' and recognised them as family.

Stories build families and communities. They transfer deep emotional knowledge between groups. If your message is true – if it is authentic, with no motive other than to inspire empathy for your experience – then audiences will take a harrowing or uplifting journey with you.

Poetry slam is live user-generated content, crowd-sourced and pushed to the top through the likes and views of a live audience. It's a democratic creative forum. It's even more accessible than the online space. It's direct and immediate. Poetry slams leap barriers. No cast. No crew. No camera. You don't even need to learn an instrument. Anyone can stand in front of a group, say what they feel and have it validated by the audience's reaction.

This is why poetry slams have become a community development and education tool. They are immediate and accessible.

Use this book as a treasure map to help you find the gold hidden inside your heart and head, then pour it out as poetry, song and stories. This is a guide that will lead you to the *X* marking the spot on the stage, behind the microphone, in the spotlight.

2
WRITE IT

When you perform poetry to a live audience, you have a direct, eye-to-eye connection with a group of people. You're not there to inform them, persuade them or deliver a speech to them. You are there to express yourself. You are offering a gift. It feels great. It feels cathartic.

It's also sheer bravery. In a live performance, you only have whatever you can do with your mouth and body. We're talking about you and your words. It's a one-person script delivered by the writer. (Group poems are great too, but we'll talk about those later – see pages 117–20.)

For now, it's all about you.

I can't tell you what words to write, but I can help you craft a poem that kickstarts an audience's imagination.

Then you take this skill and apply it all over the place – in presentations, articles, performances, relationships. Poetry gets to that core skill – good-quality writing.

WRITE TO EMPOWER

'My Year 7 English teacher told me I should write. She saw that I got bullied, like a lot. So she gave me this notebook and told me to write it all down to help figure myself out. I got picked on throughout high school and primary school. Because I was the different-looking one, in a not too multicultural area. I'd go home and be told all these incredible stories about my ancestors and my strong Punjabi heritage ... Whereas I would go to school and I was absolutely bottom rung on the ladder. So writing was a form of empowerment. Writing was how I discovered my own voice and realised, "Oh damn! I've got something to say."'

Zohab Zee Khan,
2014 Australian Poetry Slam Champion

Ten ideas to make your writing jump

By the end of this chapter you should have at least one piece of writing. You could start this in heaps of ways: create an outline and fill it in; put a toy or a seed pod in front of you and describe it; decide that today you write about cats. I'm suggesting you start with your stream of consciousness (idea 1). From there craft a poem and create new drafts that incorporate the different ideas in order. Or write several pieces that respond to a mix of the ideas in different orders. For example, start with a turning point (idea 6) and go into metaphor (idea 5). The stream of consciousness is the pile of words. The rest of the craft is up to you.

Idea 1: Vomit onto the page

Put on an instrumental track. You don't want someone else's words creeping into your writing.

Now put your pen to the page. Move your pen across the page and make words. If you get stuck, just write, 'Nothing comes into my head. No thing come sin to my head. Not hing co mes in tom y he ad' – until something does.

This is stream-of-consciousness writing, sometimes called 'lightning writing' or 'free writing'. This is also how you get out the basic rubbish of the day and transition into your subconscious. Don't stop writing until the track finishes. If you're on a roll, keep going. Vomit your words onto the page. Tap into a deeper part of yourself. Write things you didn't know were there.

Here's an example. I write this:

Now I sit to write. This is my friend. My little flat white with no lines. Spiral spine. Black face. Gray back. Damn! Why did I decide to sit outside at this cool café when the traffic she be so strong?! Coughing in me nose, exhaust fumes, beeps blaring,

eyes itchy throat going all raspy. I persist. But now I
see why people want to become cars.

Then I get to a thought like 'People want to become cars'.
I got there by mining my surface, finding words hidden
just under my awareness.

I take that sentence and follow on:

Tinted windscreens on our eyes. Wheels on our feet.
Exhaust pipe ciggies sticking out of our mouths.
Backpack boots on our backs. We are jealous. Cars
are bigger, stronger, faster, harder. They have a larger
footpath. Aliens looking down on earth believe we
are a world of large metallic creatures with bright
shiny eyes that insert fleshy power packs before
going hunting.

Once you have a raw heave of words, you clean up the
mess, find the chunks that are still edible, compost them
back into earth, grow more food, feed it to other people
and call it 'sick poetry, bro!' Or, if you prefer garden met-
aphors: plant a bunch of seeds. Pull out the weeds. Feed
the soil. Nurture. Prune. Collect the fruit and sell it to
other people. Yum.

There's a *lot* of time between inspiration and result
… but what a delicious poem. I may be extending and
mixing these metaphors just a little further than I should.
Vomit becomes compost, compost becomes soil, soil
feeds seeds, seeds become plants, plants become food.
The writing process is just as cyclical. (Sick lick ill.)

RECORD IT

TRY THIS

So, you've pushed your pen across the page without stopping for about the length of an instrumental track. You vomited into your notebook with words.

Cool. But if your flow is too fast for your fingers ... pick up your phone. Open up your voice recording app and hit 'Record'.

A recording will also help if you have a particular way of speaking that's hard to get down on paper – a beat, an accent, volume shifts or other aspects of performance. At this stage you want to generate content.

Be sure you name your recordings right away. You can always transcribe them later for print.

Bottom line: just start writing or recording. Often. A lot. Anyone can do it. The real craft is editing later.

We need the raw explosion *and* the finished shiny fruit. Some of it you will keep. Those words in your notebook may bubble through your brain for years. You ruminate over them, editing, rewriting and eventually deciding 'this one is for performance *and* publication'. Other stuff will come out as a tirade. Exploding off the tongue. Scaring people. It may make them feel gross, inspire them to look at their own mess, encourage them to take action. It may scare *you*. It may even inspire you to take action.

For example, looking at my vomitous notebook writing above, I removed the bit about writing on the busy road and the poetic description of my notebook. I am now working on that world of large metal beasts using humans for food. This is a whole and consistent concept that came from my subconscious. Now, with my conscious editor hat on, I will apply rules to it.

Idea 2: Write a picture of action

As you look through your writing to find the best bits and convert your *blaaaah* into something legible, change concepts into actions. Use concrete language, not abstractions, symbols and clichés. The audience should be able to see the world you're creating in front of them. This is important in a live performance.

If the first sentence of your poem, story or monologue is

> I find it atrocious how unconscious society's
> revolutionaries pretend to be in this monocultural
> void of existential reality we all seem to be content
> within …

then your audience will go into their own internal monologue trying to understand your first line. They may think about it for 10 seconds, 30 seconds, 2 minutes or all the way home. ('Wow, that was deep!')

But while they're thinking about it, they're not listening. If your performance goes for 2 minutes and they miss 30 seconds of it, they just missed a quarter of your show. When they come back from that first internal thought wrestle, they'll try to pick up your thread again. If they're hit with another barrage of concepts, the same effect occurs until, by the finale, they have no real idea of what you said other than something about 'atrocious', 'unconscious', 'revolution' and 'monocultural void'. Well, we all agree with that, right? Cue: finger-snap! Finger-snap! Applause! Applause!

Instead: paint a picture of action. What does a revolution look like? What does it sound like? What does a revolutionary do? Your first thoughts might be: fist in the air, protest signs. These are clichés. Go deeper. Draw a picture of action with your words:

> Driving in a 74 Buick LeSabre dark blue
>   Delilah's got a bottle rocket for a hairpin.
> She's screaming about escaping the zoo.
> I put my face in her ear. Whisper,
> 'Monkeys been in the zoo
> so long they think it's home.'
> I say, 'Their mountain climbing is on the
>   TV screen
> and it's only safe to be a clone ...'

Where does it go from here?

Whatever it is you care about, don't just tell the audience that you're sad about it, you're happy, you're angry.

Your audience will understand that *you* feel that way. They may even agree with you in theory: 'Yeah, that's something to be angry about.'

What you want is for the *audience* to feel. That good old advice to 'show, don't tell' comes into play here.

Sad:

That's when my yellow budgie, Casey, went – smack! Mum shut the window last night.

Angry:

My brother sold my mint-condition *Daredevils*. Bought his girlfriend a jumper. She dumped him two days later. I dread the smell of ink floating from the door of Rick's One Stop Comics, 117 Electra Street. Smells of lost child.

Happy:

Keep your hand in your lap if you eat your snot. [Pause] Oh, quite a few of you. If it was today … Mmm. Interesting. In the last hour? Last minute? Yeah. I saw you.

Images of action use mostly nouns (person, place or thing) and verbs (action), with a few adjectives (description). It can be as spare as this:

Legs kick
Eyes clench
Throat tight
Your mouth is full of salt water
Gulp
One
Two

--

-

You are crushed by sea. Tying a heavy sack of
magic stones around my ankles, I dive. Deeper
than your drowning black. With a heel on my
underwater head, you step from the storm.
Healed.

Take your audience through those vivid moments that
pushed your buttons. Recreate the scene. Walk us into
the details. Catch us in the trap that scared the crap out
of you. Conjure up the experience that drove you to spit
this poetic diatribe.

Do not be didactic. Didactic writing spells things out
in a really obvious, instructive way. So, repeat after me:
'I shall not write like a patronising parent, ironing out
every nuance like a stubborn wrinkle, until my message
is stiff and flat.' You are striking a balance between get-
ting your message across and letting your audience use
their imaginations.

Visualise a spectrum of artistic expression. On one
end, you have a blank canvas hanging on a gallery wall.

ABSTRACT TO CONCRETE

TRY THIS

What do you care about? What's important to you? Just start throwing down abstract concepts, like:

- family
- love
- food
- peace
- compassion
- home

Write down your own six words, or choose from those above.

If you saw a photo of each of these things, what would the photos include? Create six images of action with your words. If you chose 'family', you might write:

> Six people sit around a wooden table full of food. Two older. Four young. Three small kids lock hands over one slice of wholemeal. Ripping it. The littlest cries. Parents shout about rent as they fork tofu. A teen's thumb bounces on his glowing phone's face. His head down; lost in likes. That's me having dinner with my fam; stuck in phone land.

Your turn ...

At this end of the spectrum, the artist is saying, 'You have to give 100 per cent to this. Make it up.' Then, at the other extreme, is the B-grade Hollywood action movie. Gives you everything. It's so over the top that you can sit back and let the movie do all the work for you. It's like: *I paid my money. I just want to be entertained. Gimme 110 per cent. I'm taking a break from thinking.*

Some poetry is full of riddles, references to classical Greek myths, a bit of Nietzsche. The audience can feel alienated and confused, and discouraged from going on the journey. Other poems are pop jingles, or they're 'This is how we brush our teeth properly. Now you try!' poems.

The best work moves between 60:40 and 40:60 in the blank-canvas to hit-me-over-the-head-Hollywood ratio. It's when the artist gives just enough for the audience to engage, invest and fill in the picture with their own imaginations. You want your listener/viewer/reader to be inspired to discover the meaning. It's like inviting a friend to cook a meal with you instead of ordering them takeaway wrapped in plastic. Go further: invite them to pick some greens from your garden, bring some ingredients and mix their stock into your stew.

Idea 3: Six senses

Describe experiences using your physical senses. This is where you add juicy adjectives (describing words). Be concise and vivid with your *emerald* meadows, *prune* fingertips and *crunchy* forest floors.

What did you see, hear, touch?

We can only know the world through our senses. If you want to teleport your audience, sensory references are the way to do it.

Smell and taste are pretty neglected. If you *really* want your audience to wake up in the realm you've built, include these two senses – the sniffing and salivating. They are much more personal.

You need to observe from the inside out. Call all of your senses to attention when you're working to transfer an experience to others. Visceral action stimulates our emotions.

Bring your audience into the world you are creating. They know the stench of sweat, the itchy armpits, the taste of garlic more clearly than they know what fear means to you. When you say 'I was scared', your listener understands that you were frightened. But when you lay out how each specific image and action awakened each of your senses, the audience becomes frightened too. They don't simply nod their heads in agreement, thinking, 'Yes, that must have been very alarming for you. Go on.' They squeal, they sweat, they clutch the armrest. They lean forward ready to run. They think the knife is coming for them.

After you have layered your story with sights, sounds, smells, tastes and scratchy wool on your inner thighs, turn to the sixth sense: your imagination.

What was the moment like from the dog's perspective? What did the man at the petrol station see? What did the brick taste like?

ACTIVE LISTENERS

At Verses Festival of Words, and at the Edmonton Poetry Festival in Canada, the host of each poetry event would come out say as part of their Acknowledgment of Country and other introductory bits, 'We understand that poetry and storytelling can bring up difficult emotions for people. So we have three volunteer listeners in the room with glow sticks around their necks. If at any point you feel you need to talk with someone for any reason, you can approach one of our "active listeners", step outside the venue with them and talk with them about how you're feeling.'

I thought this was one of the most inclusive approaches to an event I've ever witnessed. It covers any possible trigger-warning message. I cry when people talk about helicopters because two very close friends of mine died in a helicopter. But you would never start your poem with, 'Trigger warning. This poem is about helicopters.'

We're often told to write what we know. This doesn't mean you can't write about dragons. Just describe the dragon blowing flames in exactly the way your grandmother blows on a cup of Earl Grey tea, something you have watched all your life. This will give people a very

TRY THIS

SENSORY REWRITE

You know all those abstract concepts we turned into images and actions back in idea 2 (page 27)? Rewrite those bits and, this time, awaken each sense. Use every sense in your retelling.

realistic picture of your fantasy creature. Be sure to add the sulphuric smell of your granny's silent but deadly gas leaks to her puff of tea steam and puckered, cherry-stained lips before the she-dragon unleashes her brimstone fire blast.

Observe your world closely. Then slide it into the multicoloured envelope of imagination where any world is possible.

Idea 4: Cut unnecessary words

If you think your ideas are important enough to write down, why start your poem with ...

[drum roll] ...

'The'

or [trumpet fanfare] ...

'A'

?

When you write poetry, always question adverbs, adjectives, prepositions, articles (*the, a, an*) and conjunctions (linking words like *and, but, because, or, often*). Try to change or edit out words like *this, there* and *that*. Write using verbs, nouns and a light peppering of adjectives. Remember, you need images of action:

- images = nouns + adjectives
- action = verbs.

Frangipani rustles. Branches snap. Clouds kick. Lightning
Noun   Verb   Noun   Verb   Noun   Verb   Noun

zips. Chimney explodes.
Verb   Noun   Verb

Brick shards shower our barbecue. Kids cry. Cake
Adj.   Noun   Verb   Pronoun   Noun   Noun   Verb   Noun

flattened. Party cancelled.
Verb   Noun   Verb

The word 'brick' in the lines above is usually thought of as a noun. Here I've used it as an adjective to describe the shards.

Use vivid adjectives related to the senses, like we spoke about in idea 3 (page 32). Just don't stack a bunch of adjectives in front of a noun. No lists please, e.g. ... *the blue, hard, large, chipped, egg-shaped marble* ... Nope. Not working.

As I wrote the above noun/verb sentences, I originally wrote, 'Kids cry over flattened cake.' This still would have been a strong line. The preposition *over* puts the kids' crying in direct relationship to the flattened cake. Where and why are they crying? Over the cake. But to keep the same formula of nouns and verbs I edited the phrase into the two sentences you see.

A preposition usually tells us where things (nouns) are in relation to each other. What is their position (*over, under, on, in* ...), in time (*before, after, during* ...) or direction (*up, down, to, from* ...)? Cut prepositions in the editing process. Add them back in if you just can't get a powerful sentence without them.

Try to cut adverbs. Adverbs are words that modify verbs. Most*ly* they are words ending in *–ly*: quickly, angrily, wickedly, ignorantly. Notice how these sharp verbs sound softer with the *–ly* suffix. Think about this sentence with its adverbs:

Her anger twists wickedly and ignorantly into joy.

Compare it to:

Her anger twists into wicked ignorant joy.

It's a subtle difference but the second one is more powerful. The first one modifies how her anger twists. The second one creates a new type of joy.

Adverbs can also work to point out the time (*now*), the location (*here*) or the extent of the action (*often*).

All these words can weaken your impact. They take up space. Remember our chat about creating images of action? The rule you should return to is 'Cut where you can'.

Here's an example of what I mean. Which of these two stories is more compelling when performed?

Story 1: The Rock Rolls Down the Hill

There once was a rock that sat on the top of a hill. It was hit by all kinds of weather: rain, snow, sun and lightning. One day, because of erosion, it began to roll down the hill. Slowly, at first, then it began to pick up speed. Meanwhile, a car was driving down the highway near the hill. The rock kept rolling and the car kept driving. Eventually the rock reached the bottom of the hill at the same time as the car. The rock landed on the roof of the vehicle. Everyone got out and ran from the automobile. Then they checked to make sure everyone was okay. Luckily no one was hurt. The end.

[116 words]

Story 2: Rock Rolls

Rock. [*Hold up your right fist*] Tumble tumble. [*Twist your fist around and bring it down*] Tumble. Tumble. Lamborghini vroooommmmm! [*Your left*

hand is flat and moves in a zigzag by your left side.]
Tumble, tumble. Vrooooommmm! Tumble. [*Two
hands hit each other with a clap*] Crashhh! Bang!
Aaahhh! [*Run across stage; look around*] You okay?
… Phew!

[17 words; mostly onomatopoeia or vocal sound
effects]

TRY THIS

CHOP CHOP

Editing is key to your craft. Cut and rebuild.

Edit your important ideas and sensorial descriptions
down to mostly images of action. If you've been
scribbling your way through all the previous 'Try This'
prompts, you should have a pile of ideas you think
are important, and you will have added a bunch of
descriptions that use the senses to take us into your
world. Now it's time to chisel.

Go through your text. Circle all the nouns and verbs.
Rewrite them on a new sheet.

Or go through and chop. Find adverbs (words
ending in *–ly*), articles (*the, a, an*), conjunctions (*and,
but, because, however, so* …) and prepositions. Cut
these as much as you can. What you have left should be
rich and vivid language.

You are writing a script, so write what you will perform. Include blocking – the movement and stage directions, shown in brackets above – where you need to. Think about *how* you will perform your work on stage, in front of an audience or on camera.

Idea 5: Metaphor is message

If you're trying to get a political point across, don't become a talking-head preacher. Your poem or story is a metaphor. It *represents* your message through a journey.

Metaphors and similes are figures of speech that we use in sentences to describe things and actions.

Simile:
Her skin is *like* molasses.

Metaphor:
Her skin *is* molasses.

But when we talk about an entire poem or story as a metaphor, we mean that the entire work symbolises or represents something else. It's also called an analogy.

If I want to write about immigration, I write about pigeons. I talk about birds migrating or staying in the cold; there are images of overcrowding, diversity, feeding, flight and beauty. I don't just come out and say 'Treat undocumented migrants more humanely'.

When you express a poem as an opinion, your audience gets the chance to disagree with you. Take them on a journey, a story with a message embedded inside it, where they can identify with the experiences of the main character. They'll come out of the poem with more empathy for your point of view. They may even question their own behaviour: 'Hmm ... maybe I *am* racist ...'

The simplest example of story-as-metaphor is found in fables. A fable tells a story and, at the end, usually sums up a direct moral or lesson the writer believes that the audience should take from the story.

Aesop was an Ancient Greek storyteller known for his fables. In his fable *The Boy who Cried Wolf*, a shepherd shouts 'Wolf!' as a joke, and people come running to help. The shepherd laughs. The people leave. The boy cries 'Wolf!' again, and the same thing happens. Then a wolf comes. The shepherd shouts for a third time. Everyone ignores him. The sheep and the boy are eaten. The message is that if you tell lies, people won't trust you when you need them to believe you.

Stories work as metaphors in movies, too. Here's one: a guy works in a factory. He's fired, the workers go on strike, the guy goes off to fight in the war. Our guy loses his leg, comes home, becomes homeless, turns into an alcoholic. A woman he knew at school sees him, takes him in and tries to help. He can't be helped. The woman gets cancer. The guy steps up to save her. He quits drinking and gets a job. They fall in love. She dies. He seeks out the family he's avoided for ten years.

You walk out of the cinema saying to yourself, 'Maybe I do support unions. War is bad. Homeless people need help. Alcoholics need love. You know, even

WHAT'S A METAPHOR FOR?

TRY THIS

Take the images of action you've been crafting and turn them into a metaphor for something you think is important. For this exercise, just pick one message related to your important idea – family, peace, home, or whatever idea you've chosen – then construct an analogy that illustrates it.

For example, here's one about the idea of justice:

> A village wakes before dawn. Elders gather in a boy's room. Last night's cedar fire smoked a rind into their wool shirts. His nostrils wake before his eyes. Sandpaper hands rub his arms. They shake him from bed. He doesn't kick. They walk him to the cliff edge of town. Bow heads. Close eyes. One raisin-faced woman steps forward, eyes wide, humming a melody. She pushes him. They all turn their backs. He doesn't scream. A couple sob and sniff back thick mucus. They shuffle home in vanishing darkness. First sunlight stretches up white stone steps hitting grey columns.

It's dark, yes, but that's just one idea for how justice could be displayed in narrative, poetic form.

What's important to you? Sport – weightlifting? The internet – trolling? Your dog – what breed? And do you pick up its poo *every* time? Or chocolate – dark chocolate with almonds? Individually wrapped mini bars of super-sweet nougat flakes, coated in milk chocolate? Raw cacao?

Be specific. Details carry meaning and symbolism. Stretch your ideas into something universal. You think chocolate is the most important thing in this solar system but how is a cheap chocolate bar different from a cacao-coated goji berry? Those two things represent very different ends of the chocolate spectrum and might reflect very different world views.

jerks can turn their lives around when they are needed.' Yet the actors didn't turn to the camera and say 'War bad!' or 'Help the homeless!' In the best scripts, actors don't deliver takeaway messages.

This is the same with you performing your poetry. Don't let the audience know that you're persuading them towards your views on climate change until it's too late. They laugh. They cry. They applaud. They suddenly realise, 'Hey, she's talking about me. Am I really like that? I *can* go a month without plastic.'

You can always find a room full of people who agree with you and who will cheer you on. It's called 'preaching to the converted'. It feels great. You walk away feeling empowered in your opinions. The real trick is how to change the minds of people outside your own community.

With your writing, the audience steps inside the character. Then the character disappears, and so do you. You become a human-shaped vessel for carrying stories, and each person in the audience sees themselves moving through the conflicts and resolutions as you express them. Each audience member goes on a journey, and that journey hopefully changes them. They are taken to the intense point that inspired your opinion. They are left to make choices. Would *they* help a homeless person?

We are all the heroes of our own stories. Even if others see us as villains.

Idea 6: Your turning points

This is one of the most important bits. Take moments from your own life when everything changed and put them in your writing. A turning point can be as simple as the first time you rode a bicycle on your own. It can be as complicated as the moment you realised your dad was gone.

If nothing changes, nothing happens. You have no story. Simple. Pick a very specific moment when your world changed and expand out from there. You'll find your deepest emotions locked within these moments. Use fine detail. Your experience has universal significance. Start with your personal experience and ask: *How is this like what other people go through?*

In a high school workshop, I ask people to write about a moment when everything changed. Here's an example of the kind of response I occasionally get: 'My parents got divorced. I cried. I was very upset. It was very sad. That was the moment when everything changed.'

I feel like that isn't enough depth for something so powerful, something that many of us have experienced. I've created the following conversation from lots of people's responses over a decade of pushing for people to describe a turning point using their senses.

I ask, 'Where were you when found out?'

'I was watching TV.'

'Then what happened?'

'I heard my dad crying in the kitchen.'

'What did you do?'

'I went in and saw him.'

'What did you see?'

'He looked like he was holding himself up. Leaning over the bench. His shoulders were lifting up and down and I could hear him kind of sobbing. I said, "Daddy, what's wrong?" He turned to me and it was like his legs folded. He dropped down onto his knees. He reached out and touched my face. Then put his head down. He leaned into me.'

'Do you remember what he smelled like?'

'His hair smelled salty and sweet. Kind of like the beach. I hugged him. He said, "You're coming to live with me." I saw in my head our happiest times together with Mum at the beach.'

As hard as it is to face a memory like that, these kinds of experiences will move anyone who listens. They will immediately feel what you went through. Any group of keen listeners will feel its punch.

A writer is able to process difficult emotions through creativity and active self-expression. The person telling this story now has an external reference that allows them to put some distance between themselves and the pain of that moment. In time, this process can help to heal the turmoil of unspent emotion that gets locked away sometimes after trauma. This guide is about writing and performance, not about mental health, but we have to acknowledge the powerful effect art can have on personality and sense of wellbeing. It's empowering to feel heard. The spoken word community in Australia is really supportive. They will applaud you, welcome you and make you feel at home. Those ideas and experiences

POSITIVE EFFECTS

'Participating in the Australian Poetry Slam was truly a rewarding and uplifting experience for me. When the [state] heats rolled around, I was working hard to try and lift myself out of a fairly serious mental and emotional slump. To make it to the National Final had a significant, positive impact on my life, and has helped to give me the confidence and motivation to pursue other endeavours.'

Sarah Jane Justice, 2018 Australian Poetry Slam National Finalist

TRY THIS

CHANGE IT UP

Choose a moment in your life when everything changed. Describe it through your senses using mostly images and actions. Then tell us what it says about the world – i.e. turn it into a metaphor.

you thought were 'weird'? Share them with a group of friends first to build up your confidence in creative self-expression. Then try it out on stage.

While the process of writing through trauma can be a healthy experience, the emotional release can be hard to deal with on your own. If tapping into the past feels too painful, make sure you seek the support of a professional counsellor, a therapist or, at minimum, a close friend to help you navigate this territory.

Idea 7: Perspectives and tenses

For a live performance, the most powerful writing is in first person and present tense. *I* am talking. This *is* happening *right now*.

First, second and third person

In **first person,** the person speaking is telling their story. The personal pronouns you use in first-person writing are *I, me, my, we* and *us.* This will give your work immediacy, intimacy and authenticity.

(Note: Ever noticed how many brands incorporate these first-person pronouns? There's iPhone, YouTube, Wii, My School, MyGov and MyBank for starters. Even countries can have pronoun brands, like the U.S. Makes me wonder who T.H.E.Y. are ...)

In **second person,** the writer speaks directly to the reader or listener. The personal pronoun here is *you*: 'You sit on the couch reading this book. You sip your apple juice. You turn the page.'

In **third person,** the personal pronouns are *he/him, she/her* and *they/them.* If you've ever written a bio for yourself, and your name is Marsha Latrec (totally made-up name), you might write: 'Marsha Latrec enjoys working on spreadsheets. She creates pie charts for fun. When Marsha isn't entering data, she likes to eat raw cacao goji berries.'

Past, present and future tense

Now, you must know about **past, present** and **future tenses,** right? As I said, the best one for performing live in front of folks is present tense: 'I am here now.' Look at these examples:

- Present tense: 'I *run* to the store. I *see* a dinosaur.'
- Past tense: I *ran* to the store. I *saw* a dinosaur.'

- Future tense: 'I *will run* to the store. I *will see* a dinosaur.'

Sometimes you can do the tricky **present continuous** or **future continuous,** which just means you add an *–ing* to a verb, and an extra word or two:

- Present continuous: I *am running* to the shops.
- Future continuous: I *will be running* to the shops.

Now mix first and second person in present tense and the whole room transforms: 'You are here with me. I am talking to you there in the front row.' This does not mean that you are only speaking autobiographically. For example:

I plead from my passenger's pew looking at you.

You refuse to sit next to me for fear of eau de human.

In this instance, the writer is a person on a bus. Audience members are passengers. The space the writer performs in is transformed into a crowded bus and the performer sits in an empty seat in the crowd. Audience members are addressed directly. They are now sitting with:

Old smelly pants, the amusing little reminder of what we're all like under our perfumed cells.

Alternatively, if you write in past tense, your performance will have a 'storytelling' feel:

> This happened a long long time ago in a Galaxy Car Wash far far away from Parramatta.

For this you will need a strong narrative, a confident stage presence and compelling action. The audience is much more detached and prone to get distracted by their brain's own internal chatter if your piece is set in the past and is about 'her' or 'them'.

Thankfully, good stories have beginning, middle and end points. As listeners our thoughts can dip out and back in again. As the action intensifies, conflict builds and the direction turns; a cheeky audience member looks up from their phone, stunned to attention.

If you're writing in past tense, a great way to create immediacy is to set the scene. Where are we? Take us there.

Also take on several character voices throughout (see idea 8, below). Interspersing dialogue brings us into the present, even if the story happened many many seconds ago:

> I was working in this café, right? Over on
> Devonshire Street. This place got about
> 15 customers in 8 hours. Manager walks in.
> *Yo' mister big man, wasup?*

FIRST PERSON PRESENTS ...

TRY THIS

I'm assuming you've been stopping and crafting a new poem as you read this. If not, that's cool. Take anything you've written or recorded at any time. Play with it. Change tense from past to present to future. Try speaking it in a different voice – deeper or shrill, accented, slow, thick, quick. Change from *I* to *he* to *you*. Speak these changes aloud. How do they feel? How do they change the mood and impact of your piece?

Idea 8: Characters and voice

Some writers have a fixed idea of what a 'slam voice' sounds like. They think of poems about identity politics performed with a certain rhythmic cadence and wild gesturing. But if this was the only style of poetry performed by 20 different artists in one night, it would become tiresome halfway in. Those who break from this stereotype stand out.

Write characters

A great way to make your writing stand out is to experiment with writing as a character. Try writing in several different voices, dialects and accents. If you are writing about a moment in your own life, pick someone or

FIND YOUR VOICE

'One thing I'd like to see change is the imitation of the American slam style, which has a very recognisable cadence and delivery style. I'd love to see emerging Australian poets carve out their own unique styles and discover their own voices. This to me is far more exciting than an imitation of a style that sounds predictable and tired ... to me anyway!'

Candy Royalle, poet and activist

something else in the scene and write with their voice. No one is saying you need to be a trained actor to perform your writing, but having the ability to change your voice, stance, gestures and facial expressions will enhance your writing and add to your performance. You'll be able to retell conversations, add dialogues and tri-alogues (not sure if that's a word). You are writing a script for one. (Ensemble pieces are great too. We'll get to those later.)

And if you want to represent the way that people really speak, your powers of observation will be crucial.

Listen to people. On a long train ride on the North Island of New Zealand, I was writing fiction when I overheard a woman say to her partner, 'You know how when ya like eat a curry and then you have like a ginger beer and then ya burp and it's like spicy? I like that.' I had to use it for one of the characters in my story. It felt like a line I could never have made up.

Write your own dialect

At the same time, don't be afraid to use your own way of speaking. You should know that your 'slang' with your mates is a language as well. Linguists say so. For example, the way African–Americans speak is a language/dialect called Ebonics or African–American Vernacular English (AAVE). If you can master 'proper' English and write in your own dialect, you are preserving a unique document of your local culture's speech patterns. When you choose between the two modes – educated and slang – you're doing something called 'code switching'. You speak one way with your nanna, another with your friends, another with your school principal and another with your work colleagues.

It is good to have the choice, though. Learn English, keep your own language or dialect and learn other languages so you can choose when you'd like to speak to 'doze guys over dere', 'these people over here' and *'estas personas aquí'*.

Maxine Beneba Clarke talked with me about using accents that relate to her cultural roots and lineage. She says that she doesn't use the accents from her family heritage very often, and that she'd be reluctant to perform in someone else's accent. 'It's not a massive part of my work but I take on another voice in some of the pieces that I do. I think I've written five poems that way in my life,' she says. 'The only accented English that I'm comfortable performing in is Caribbean Diaspora accented English, because I grew up around it. That's the accent my parents used to have. That's the accent that my grandparents, my cousins had. That's the only accent that's taken from my cultural heritage. And I wouldn't feel confident doing that if I didn't have experience with that kind of accented English.'

Beware cultural appropriation and imitation

For people whose cultures have suffered severe oppression, hearing an imitation of their accent or characteristics can be traumatising for them. In some cases their ancestors have been dehumanised, enslaved or forced to flee their homelands. To dress up and try to imitate their accents or mannerisms is insensitive. Parodies of other people's dialects in these cases are at best disrespectful, and at worst racist and cruel.

Be aware of the power imbalances before you create these characters. If a dominant majority group imitates a minority group, the offensiveness is compounded. So, yes it feels okay to mimic a posh English accent. The upper-class English culture has certain privileges attached to it, and while imitating it does perpetuate stereotypes, it is not the same as ridiculing the accent of a culture that has been oppressed or marginalised. It feels okay to imitate the oppressor or coloniser, not the oppressed or colonised. Always check your characters are not demoralising or disadvantaging any particular group.

STOP THE STEREOTYPES

I once watched a group of pre-teens dance in a school talent show. They danced to a Michael Jackson song wearing big black afro wigs. Almost all of the kids were Anglo-European. This offended me. Being African–American, I've seen people parody the horror of slavery, acting it out in old vaudeville shows and films from before 1940. These were called 'minstrel shows' and featured white people wearing brown or black face make-up. The African–American characters were portrayed as uneducated and inhuman and their pain was mocked.

I am nothing like these characters. Or any stereotype referenced by an afro wig. Same goes for references to watermelon, basketball and even 'You perform poetry. You mean you rap?' When I see white people dressing up as black people I feel like the pain of my ancestors is being ridiculed. I feel like my individual personal identity – with all of my unique quirks, behaviours, beliefs and interests – is being disregarded.

This would apply to parodies of many other people – like victims of the Holocaust or genocide in Cambodia, or the indigenous peoples of many nations, or refugees, or any people who have been systematically traumatised and disempowered. They don't need entertainment to rub salt into their wounds.

MILES

TRY THIS

LISTEN AND LEARN

Next time you're on public transport or in a café and hear an interesting conversation or just an accent, notice how many times 'like', 'you know' and 'mmm' come up.

Record some of your own conversations. (Let the person/people you're speaking with know you're recording them, of course.)

Not only will you get a clearer idea of how people really speak, you may get inspiration from the content.

Make an effort to meet people from cultures you have an interest in. Find out about their lives, suggest a collaborative poem or story, or invite them to perform themselves.

When it comes down to it, if you're going to imitate or parody an identity, it's best to use your own. If you want to go outside of your own cultural identity, have a chat with some people from the country, language group, social group or ancestry you want represent. Talk to them about your plan. See what they think. Listen to them. Seek their guidance before trying to speak as them. Make new friends.

Empower others

It's also better to find ways to empower previously oppressed people to tell their own stories than trying to tell their stories for them and gaining applause for yourself. If you want to tell another person's story of injustice as a way of bringing attention to their plight, go out and meet the people you want to support, talk with them and collaborate with them. At the very least, get permission to repeat their stories. An even better approach is to help give *them* a platform to speak up.

Being able to speak in front of a group gives you an opportunity to bring attention to an oppressed people's history and struggle. Just learn when to step aside and hand them the mic.

Idea 9: Rhythm, metre, rhyme

When we think of poetry, we often think it must be a piece of writing with a structured rhythm. I've been told, dozens of times, 'That's not real poetry. How can you call it poem if it doesn't rhyme?' – as though the canon of classic poetry is made entirely of rhyming couplets.

My response is: 'I don't know. Ask Robert Frost, TS Eliot, Langston Hughes, Sylvia Plath. Or Australian poets: Les Murray, Dorothy Porter, Gwen Harwood, Oodgeroo Noonuccal.' These are people we think of as being part of that list called 'The Greatest Poets, Like, Everrr'. They all write in **free verse**. So do thousands of other poets.

Free verse

Free verse is just poetry without a regular rhyme scheme, a regular rhythm or a formal structure. It is this anti-form that most poets today write in. The idea is that what's in the poem – its content – should take priority over its structure.

Let's turn this question inside out. If you spit out clichés, stats, facts and flat statements in rhyming couplets, does that make it poetry? If you speak them to a beat, does that make them rap? I guess. But do I want to listen to it? Nope.

Most poetry of the 20th and 21st centuries is written in free verse. If a poet today rhymes the end words of every second sentence, it's usually kinda crap. The rhythm gets dull. The lines can feel forced into an uncomfortable jacket. If you do use rhyme, try not to emphasise the end-of-line rhyming words when performing. It starts to feel sing-songy and repetitive.

Sometimes rhyme works. I throw in bouncy rhymes when I'm performing for primary school students. If you are writing a song, or keeping to a particular beat in accompanying music, then go for it. A songwriter can create a masterpiece with rhyme, but turn off the music and the effect is usually lost.

There are some exceptions, but powerful poetry for performance flows like a conversation. There are some rhymes and rhythms embedded in a free-verse poem, but nothing that has a continuous pattern throughout.

If you do want to use rhyme and rhythm …

Okay, now I've ranted enough about the anti-rhyme.

There *are* poets who count syllables and match up sentence structures in stanzas and verses. They spit rhyme schemes and even use the classic **iambic pentameter** (see the box on page 64 for a little iambic instruction). You can watch 12 Australian Poetry Slam champions (www. australianpoetryslam.com/champions) to see how each of them uses rhyme in their own way.

Jesse Oliver, in his poem 'Dream Revolution', has lines like:

> I saw
> our native people silenced
> and seldom ever seen
> I saw refugees drowning
> off the coast in western seas
> I saw animals fleeing scenes
> from where we've cut down all their trees
> I see the men and the women
> and those that are in between
> seeing this government on standby
> that's haunting all our dreams

Phil Wilcox even plays with the notion of rhyming in his poem 'This Microphone Only Tells the Truth':

> ... the girl in the front row – she's kind of cute.
> I'm gonna assume your name is Ruth
> because it rhymes with:
> This microphone only tells the truth.

This is also where we can mention a few other techniques for playing with sound.

Alliteration means repeating the first letter of words:

> Find your friends from a field of fiends.

Assonance means repeating similar vowel sounds in words that are close together:

> My mate drank flat ginger-ale.
> Now his face is grey and pale.

Consonance is repeating similar consonant sounds in words that are close together.

> Collecting kickbacks takes a tricky knack.

Try out a variety of poetic styles to stretch your writing. Think about it like this. If an abstract painter learns figure drawing and other more formal practices, then decides to throw buckets of paint on the canvas, they have made a choice. They have the skills to create a variety of forms. They can express whatever image they have in their head as artwork. But they have *chosen* to express themselves in abstract paint splatters. If they just throw the paint, without any understanding of the art form, it's not really a choice. It's a limitation. It's all they can do.

Don't let your first style be your last layer. This is just your instigator. Go test out all the forms:

- A **sonnet** is a rhyming verse form that has 14 lines of iambic pentameter (see box on page 64). Shakespeare's sonnets follow the rhyming pattern *abab cdcd efef gg*.
- A **villanelle** is a verse of 19 lines with five three-line **stanzas** (little blocks of verse) followed by a final four-line stanza (also known as a **quatrain**). There are only two rhymes used, and some lines are repeated throughout the poem. Check out Dylan Thomas and his 'Do Not Go Gentle into That Good Night' poem for the most famous example of a villanelle.
- A **haiku** is a three-line poem with a total of 17 syllables: 5 syllables in the first line, 7 in the second and 5 in the third line. Haikus originated in Japan. They try to capture one emotion or image. Traditionally haikus include a reference to a season. The first lines flow, then they hit against a contrasting, abrupt last line.

Rhythm, rhyme and speaking to a beat: this is where poetry mirrors song lyrics. When lyricists write with music, they will often look at stressed and unstressed syllables to figure out the beats in a line.

The following four lines each have four **syllables** (individual sounds), which could equal four beats. But for rhythm you want to pay attention to the **stressed** (strong) and **unstressed** (weak) syllables in a line. That will give your writing flow. The stressed syllables have a forward slash over them – they have a '*Ta*' sound. The unstressed or weak syllables have a hook above them (called a 'breve') and have a 'tum' sound. These are the beats. Say these out loud. Depending on where you place the emphasis, each has a slightly different meaning.

/ ˘ / ˘

Have – you – heard – cows? = *Ta* tum *Ta* tum

˘ / ˘ /

Have – you – heard – cows? = tum *Ta* tum *Ta*

/ / ˘ ˘

Have – you – heard – cows? = *Ta* *Ta* tum tum

˘ ˘ / /

Have – you – heard – cows? = tum tum *Ta* *Ta*

Now let's flow this into a catchy toddler ditty:

> Have you heard cows
> Go for a browse?
> They nibble toes
> And garden hose.
> Quick! Guard your nose.

You can see how each line has a different rhythm, even though they all have four syllables in them. It all depends on which syllables you choose to emphasise.

Studying the rhythm of your text and marking the stress patterns is called **scansion**. You can do it with any text, not just rhyming poems. Scansion notation can look like the forward slashes and breves I've used above, and here:

> / ˘ / / ˘ / ˘ /
> You can do it with any text = *Ta* tum *Ta*
> *Ta* tum *Ta* tum *Ta*

This kind of notation is most helpful if you're working with musicians. They will want to play to a rhythm. There is music in what you write. This method is how you find it and show it to someone with a bass. The best performances with musicians work like the score of a film. So instead of trying to keep to the beat, the musician/s create a mood or atmosphere that can sound like

IAMBIC PENTAMETER

As we talked about on the previous pages, in any sentence you've got stressed syllables and unstressed syllables. A pair of these syllables is called an **iamb**. Like this:

˘ /

Ba boom!

Five of these pairs makes a **pentameter**. *Penta* just means five – you know, like pentagon and pentagram. Metre is the system of beats. So iambic pentameter is a rhythm with five beats per line.

Most of Shakespeare's plays and poems are written to this rhythm, like this line from the play *Twelfth Night*:

˘ / ˘ / ˘ / ˘ / ˘ /

If music be the food of love, play on

IAMBIC TETRAMETER

The iambic tetrameter has four beats per line. Iambic tetrameter is poetry-speak for the 4/4 beat you hear in nearly every pop song: think Aretha Franklin, The Beatles, Ed Sheeran ...

an ambient soundscape, a jazzy improvisation with lots of space or a bopping dance track. Ultimately you want something that doesn't require you, the writer, to keep 4/4 time in the key of C. You just want to tell a story with an emotive soundtrack. This can also come from collaborating with a DJ.

Having a bit of deep knowledge to draw from is always a good start when it comes to forms of writing. Study a bit more. Dig. Go on a treasure hunt. Learn what a villanelle is. Enter a sonnet slam. You have to learn to pluck the guitar strings before you improvise a rhythm on the guitar body with your palm, just as the abstract painter mentioned earlier needs to learn the techniques before choosing to throw paint around. If you don't have the knowledge of the foundations, you have no choice but improvisation. It will limit you. Your aim is to transfer what's in your head into the most vivid form you can choose.

One more aspect of writing to a rhythm is **pace**. Writers speed up, slow down, drop pellets of silence and create an audio rollercoaster to make crowds scream on the big loop.

Don't forget the content

A reminder: focus on content first. *Then* consider whether rhythm, rhyme, alliteration and assonance have a place in the piece. I never want the audience to be bobbing their head to the beat no matter what I say. Imagine a mad throng bouncing to a repetitive, 'Buy my merch! Buy my merch! Buy my merch!' or 'War is best!' just because it's got a killer bassline. I meet writers who come from the hip-hop community to poetry. They often say they like it when the beat cuts out and their content really counts.

Australian lyricists like Paul Kelly, Briggs, Holly Throsby, Archie Roach, Vance Joy, Sia and others create rich lyrical content that works with or without their brilliant music. Their words could be spoken as poetry and audiences would still respond because they tell great stories, avoid clichés and can perform a conversation to a beat. They don't just fit awkward rhymes into every line so they can keep time.

At the Uptown Poetry Slam at the Green Mill (see pages 8–9) they play a game called Guess the Rhyme. If you can guess the rhyme before the poet says it, you shout it out. The message is: don't be predictable.

> They're not calling you a jerk
> Just saying that your poetry needs more ...

Idea 10: Authenticity and vulnerability

Remember authenticity is key. You are not an actor. This is *your* writing.

Characters and voices are fine but you must be sincere. Your audience knows when you are not committed to the work. Tap into your raw and the audience will go there with you.

Think of an associative experience – a moment when you experienced an intense emotion, laughter, tears, shouting – and let that feed your performance. Was it an

SHORT FORM

TRY THIS

Break into your brain and rewire it for four short poems. You might not like the result but you are limbering up. You are digging in and challenging yourself. Look each of these up and write:

- a sonnet
- a villanelle
- a haiku
- a rondeau.

Extra challenge: look up a sestina and try that too.

argument with your parents? The day you won a swimming race? The new pet that died in your arms? Then take the emotion and apply it to another situation.

This idea is directly related to those turning points we discussed previously. Often the associative experience is what compelled you to create the work in the first place. It's what drove you to put black letters on to a white space. If you are a writer of the disciplined variety – you do it every day – then you have to draw on a backstory that moves you. Find something you honestly care about and ask yourself, 'Why do I care?' Our strongest opinions are based on a real thing happening. Start with the truth of your own experience.

And don't be afraid to be vulnerable. Vulnerability reads as humanity and bravery on stage. You're telling the audience how deeply they are allowed to dig into their own emotions.

In a recent workshop with Year 7 students, I asked one student to tell me about a moment in his life when everything changed. He said, 'My dog … I was holding him … when …' The student began crying.

I said, 'It's okay. Let it out. This is a safe space. Sharing your emotions is what this is all about.'

His friend patted him on the back and said, 'It's okay, mate. We're here for you.'

'What happened when you were holding your dog?' I asked.

The boy said, 'He died in my arms. He was looking at me and then he just stopped moving.'

'It's okay. We're going to get through this,' I said. 'Use this experience. Write about it. Tell it and eventually the pain will get easier. You'll get some distance from the pain just through telling your story. Take your personal story and expand it out into how we treat our animals as family.'

When it came time to perform, the young poet got on stage in front of about 400 parents, teachers and other students. He shared a poem about someone trapped in a cage watching their family be killed. Then the person speaking in the poem is released and allowed to walk around a field, pecking grains off the fresh grass. That's when the audience realises he's speaking as a caged chicken turned free range. Because of his intense

BE VULNERABLE

'I participated in a heat [of the Australian Poetry Slam] and did not perform well ... It was still a great experience, and I observed that the poems I liked best in the heat were a bit more raw and vulnerable. I normally write humorous poetry. I started opening myself up to getting some more vulnerable ideas onto a page. I liked what I wrote. [At another heat] I thought I'd have another go with my new poem, and I made it through to the state final. After the heat, I spoke to a few people who had similar experiences to me, and they told me how they connected with my words, and how my poem gave expression to their feelings. That was really gratifying.'

Tiffany Harris, 2018 Australian
Poetry Slam National Finalist

personal experience, the poet spoke like an expert on the emotions a battery hen might experience.

The audience was amazed by the power of this 60 seconds of performed writing and their praise was genuine. We told him he achieved something very difficult and rewarding. He had turned his personal experience into a work of art and transferred deep emotional insight to a large crowd of people.

THE PERFECT ROLE?

I started out as an actor when I was in Year 11. My drama teacher told me I could be anything – 'the next Denzel or Wesley Snipes'. But I wanted to be Tom Cruise.

When I finished school, I went for my first real audition. It was a play called *One Flew Over the Cuckoo's Nest*, based on the book of the same name.

I began reading the script and the director stopped me after a few lines.

'What are you doing?' he asked.

'I'm reading for the lead,' I said, in my deepest, most confident voice.

'I'm sorry,' he said. 'The lead is not black.'

'Well it doesn't say that in the script,' I replied.

'It's implied. The man's name is McMurphy. Therefore he must be Irish.'

'How does that explain Eddie?'

'Excuse me?' The director looked around at the three others sitting in theatre chairs next to him in the dim light. They giggled, confused.

'Eddie Murphy,' I said.

He rolled his eyes and scanned his clipboard.

'Regardless, we've got you listed as Janitor 1, Janitor 2 or The Indian Guy. Do you want a janitor role?'

That's when I thought that maybe actors are elaborate puppets for other people's ideas. My own dreams, ideas, insights, experiences and emotions would never come out if I waited for someone to cast me in the perfect role. So I switched my university major to English and focused on my writing.

Performing my own writing fills a void that acting can't. I'm able to speak with authenticity about the world I see and share it with the world. I satisfy my urges for introverted deep self-reflection and active public engagement.

MILES

AUTHENTIC MOMENTS

TRY THIS

Link key moments in your own life to create a story. Work on this until you feel you can make a universal point – a poignant idea that allows your audience to gain insight. Combine all the previous tips into your powerhouse performance.

This can start with something like that time you tripped over a kerb and knocked out a tooth. That might lead to ideas like: where do footpaths come from? Most days I could close my eyes and walk home. I know if I step on lawn I'm going off the path. Why isn't there grass everywhere? Or rubber footpaths? Would I be better in a country town? What would it be like to be blind?

You could even meet up with a person who is blind and work on a duet poem.

Recap

So by now you should have a piece of writing, or several pieces, incorporating these ten ideas.

You vomited onto the page with words, creating a stream-of-consciousness page of text.

From that text you found the kernel of an idea and changed all the abstract concepts to images and actions.

You added sensory descriptions to your idea.

You cut unnecessary words, leaving mostly nouns, verbs and a few adjectives.

You found a key story within your text that can symbolise a message that you want to get across.

You've picked a moment in your life when everything changed and used it as the turning point for your writing.

You've tried putting your writing into first person in the present tense, and experimented with other perspectives and tenses.

You added a voice that isn't your own to the text.

Then you edited for rhythm and maybe even rhyme.

You made sure you're being honest and authentic, allowing yourself to be vulnerable.

You've ripped through the paper in your pad. You've pounded the keyboard. You've tattooed something with your ideas.

It's time to own the stage.

3

PERFORM IT

AAAAAAAAH! I felt like screaming. Doesn't feel the same on the page, does it? Not satisfying at all. Did you feel it? Did you try reading it out loud? Did you have a go at replicating my emotion?

When I create work, I try to include things that can't be written down.

I like starting my show by coughing and clearing my throat. The coughing becomes rhythmic, then changes to a deep harmonic humming, a high-pitched singing note and then a buzz. My hand rises, my thumb and pointer finger extend and shake. I go silent as I snap my fingers. I then announce to the audience: 'That was a poem called "Some Sounds Cannot Be Written Down".'

Bring words to life

Any poem can be performed. It's up to you to bring it to life. There are exceptions, but poems come to life when you speak them out loud. You could even read a shopping list and keep an audience's attention just through giving a compelling performance.

Just look at all the ways you can say 'tomatoes', like *tom ate toes* (yuck!). What about all the physical things you can do with an invisible tomato? Pluck it from a plant, stomp on it, squeeze it, drink the juice, cook it, spread it ... Next on the list – eggs. (Insert chook sound here.) Crack one over an audience member's head (mime it though, right?). A dozen or six, free-range or caged? (Peck the floor.) Milk: *Walk on hands and knees. Chew cud. My ilk (moooo) squeeze. Squirt udder juice. Feed the calf.* Bread: *breed fungus in crusty sourdough rye.*

You get the point, right? Lots to play with if you've got voice and movement.

One imagination and IQ test is to give a person a paperclip, a pen and a notepad. The object is to see how many uses for a paperclip you can write down within a period of time. To me this says that you can write a poem about anything and bring it to life with a performance. You see this in improvisational theatre and comedy. Someone in the audience shouts out 'tangerine' and the next line has to include the random word, inspiring a laugh.

There is no 'page versus stage'. The writing and the performance run together – it's all in your ability to perform the words. Pick up any poem and, unless the words will only work when the poem is in the shape of a raindrop or the letters have to be spread around the page to mimic a grasshopper – a form of concrete poetry where the poem mixes with visual art and takes a shape – the work can be performed. (Even the grasshopper idea can be interpreted: hop across the stage.)

HOW DO YOU WRITE FOR PERFORMANCE?

'I'm thinking more about the sound of words, where the pauses go, what the rhythms are, and how that affects how the audience receives the poem. If I deliver this softer, if I whisper it, it's going to be received in a different way than if I yell it. It's a performance, so I really am thinking, Okay, this is what I want to say. How do I mould this so that (a) it sounds beautiful, (b) it does the writing justice, and the writing is good enough, and (c) the person sitting in that chair hopefully receives it, you know – takes it off the stage the same way I'm putting it on the stage.'

Maxine Beneba Clarke,
writer and spoken word poet

Here's a poem that can have a totally different meaning on paper than it does when spoken. Try reading it out loud as written.

Scratch My Back I kcaB yM hctarcS

Quick disguise.
Quack dees guys!
Quick! Day skies.
Quirk? Dusky eyes.
Qweek! De skies.
Quake: disc guise
Quit, dusk highs
Quiet, dust ties
Quikey! Disco use.
Qui K. Digs ice.
Click. Dies. Geese.

This poem has many variations using the sound of the words 'quick disguise'. On paper, you can see the different words and guess their meaning. Words are manipulated through just changing a vowel sound or adding a consonant, making use of various forms of English spoken around the world. I chose the Arial typeface because I want capital 'I' to look like a dividing line between the mirror-image words in the title.

As part of a troupe of three actors, I toured to schools performing classic poems from the New South Wales high school syllabus, like 'The Violets' by Australian

Gwen Harwood, and 'Dulce et Decorum Est' by the English World War I poet Wilfred Owen. We broke poems up into parts, with each actor trading lines back and forth. We underlined words to be said together and circled words or lines to echo. We would slow down, speed up, accentuate sorrow, emphasise jokes and generally dramatise the poems. For many of the students, these poems were nothing more than texts in books on shelves in the school library. They had not heard them aloud before we spoke them directly into their eyes and ears that day.

Try speaking the following out loud while tapping your foot on the floor or your palm on the table.

> And all should cry, Beware! Beware!
> His flashing eyes, his floating hair!
> Weave a circle round him thrice,
> And close your eyes with holy dread
> For he on honey-dew hath fed,
> And drunk the milk of Paradise.

If you spoke it to the beat, you should have something kinda hip-hop. This is the rap of 19th-century English poet and opium addict Samuel Taylor Coleridge. (Notice the eating of 'honey-dew' and drinking 'the milk of Paradise'.)

While performing 'classic' poetry with this theatrical group, I still longed to hear poems from the students we were meeting. I felt like we were reinforcing the notion that *these* poets are the masters, the artists you should

CHOOSE POETRY

TRY THIS

Imagine a person in a more conservative time – 50, 70, 100, even 200 years ago. They could choose any number of worthy occupations. I want you to meet some friends of mine: people who chose not lawyer, plumber, accountant or nurse ... but *poet*. They would have been some super-interesting, hella brave folks. Now, they weren't all wildness and free love, but just have a look at a couple of these titles squished into dusty old poetry tomes.

- Langston Hughes (1902–67), 'Boogie: 1 A.M.'
- Emily Dickinson (1830–86), 'Wild Nights - Wild Nights!'
- William Blake (1757–1827), 'Ah! Sun-flower'
- Oodgeroo Noonuccal (1920–93), 'Assimilation – No!'

Grab a classic poem like 'The Love Song of J. Alfred Prufrock' by TS Eliot. Turn on a beat. Spit some of those old-school verses out loud. See where they take you. Go on. I see a little hip sway. Is that you dancing to lines like: '... restless nights in one-night cheap hotels / And sawdust restaurants with oyster-shells'?
You go, poet!

be revering, poring over and interpreting. Sure, study the literary canon of poems. Get fresh perspectives on writing, history and the lives of others, but don't let the canon become an unscalable tower, intimidating your own inspiration and shaking your desire to create your own amazing work.

The second-scariest thing

I was looking at a survey recently. The number two scariest thing humans can do? PUBLIC SPEAKING! Number one scariest thing? Red-back spider crawls into your ear while you sleep and ... lays eggs. Hands up those who prefer public speaking? Thought so. Gee, you're brave!

SAFE SPACES

'Participating [in spoken word] at a local level in Perth and familiarising myself with well-established artists and events gave me reason to believe I could pursue my love of the art. The local scene is a very safe and welcoming one, in which artists of all ages, walks of life and levels of experience can feel comfortable in sharing their stories.'

Neil Smith, 2018 and 2019 Australian Poetry Slam National Finalist

There are a whole bunch of guides out there on public speaking. The most basic advice I can give is get yourself up onto that stage – over and over again.

The amazing thing about a poetry slam audience is that even though there are judges chosen randomly from the crowd, they're not judgmental. Spoken word audiences are supportive and encouraging. Especially if you say, 'Hey guys, this is my first time getting up on stage with my work and ...' Be aware that some venues have a tradition of interrupting you at this point to shout: 'NEW SHIT!' or 'Virgin!' These shouts are reminders that you are part of a community and to not take yourself too seriously. It's not a hazing.

You'll start out vulnerable

Slam audiences – and, in fact most of us, when we're not faced with straight-up huge celebs – are impressed by vulnerability. The audience will back you up if you keep it sincere and vulnerable. I have seen veteran slam champions strive to recall that vulnerable raw humanness they had when they once burst into tears during a performance. Some are even training themselves to cry on cue through years of Stanislavski-style training. You will have this vulnerability when you first land on stage.

When you first try performing your writing, in the intimacy of a small or medium-sized venue, the audience will know you are brave. You have compounded the fear of speaking with the added vulnerability of sharing your personal writing. You are doing what most of the

CRYING ON CUE

Konstantin Stanislavski is credited as the founder of 'method acting'. The core idea of method acting is to tap into your own emotional memories to add depth and sincerity to your characters. For many actors – from Marlon Brando, to Scarlett Johansson, to Steve Buscemi – Stanislavski is the bomb.

audience would never dare to do. Some of the audience is just itching to get on the mic themselves. People are empathising with you; they want you to succeed. If you stumble, they will applaud, snap their fingers and say 'You got this', or 'Keep going'.

When you're starting out in a slam, remember there is no right or wrong way to do it. Just give it a go. You're not there to convince people of a particular argument. It's not an essay. It's your own creative self-expression. The judges will ask themselves: 'Was I moved? Did I laugh? Did I cry? Did I feel strongly?'

Take the audience with you

But how do you draw out those emotions from your audience?

You take them on a journey from the personal to the universal.

Imagine that your chest is a reflector. When the lights go up, you turn, face the audience and reflect the spotlight back onto each face in the room. Each person feels like the show is about *them*. They see their own glories and flaws in your story – you know, that story with a big turning point that spins the whole thing into a metaphor about how we see the world? They cheer the familiar and slowly gulp back questions like: 'Is she talking about me? Am I like that? Do I need to reconsider how I treat people who are different from me?'

This is not about you, The Poet Who Must Be Heard. Yes, sure, that feels good, but this is about the audience's experience through you. This is a gift for them: a clear reflection. That, hopefully, will inspire your listeners to change, whatever your topic is – climate change, racial equality, friendship, peace, family ...

Why not basketball?

Why not my cute fluffy dog?

Because it's never just about your dog or your basketball. When you're speaking to groups of people, they are searching for *meaning*. They'll have their own personal associations that can be exciting and visceral, like 'A cute dog bit me once while I was gardening. That's why I don't garden anymore.' And they'll be thinking about this during your entire performance ... unless you make it mean something else.

Sure, start out with high school basketball:

Dribbling, three point, all net, no rim, free throw,
Jordan's swoosh!

But don't let folks settle in. They'll drift into their own distracted memories, like: *My high school basketball team ... Aaah, those were the days! I remember when ... INTERNALMONOLOGUENOTLISTENING. What's this dude on about?*

Bring 'em back to the mic with:

Elbow to the gut, push up. Knock number 47.
Brother's on the floor. Drop this orange rubber globe
in a basket like pickin' pumpkins from dirt on a
picaninny farm. Still stuck entertaining white folks
with my physique. Gladiator style. Get me on that
debate team yo'. I'll tear up the competition with my
mind. But for now I'm just popping the rock to the
net from the line.

Get out the fears

Talk about your biggest fears. We all have fears. When I lived in Chicago, my two biggest ones were homelessness and prison. Everywhere were many black men homeless, imprisoned or, lately, dead. Kept in a three-system loop: economic, penal and punitive. All I had to do was get pulled over in the wrong neighbourhood. 'Licence please. Hmm, expired. Step out of the car ...' It happened like this three times. Once I had my car taken from me for an indicator light that was 'irregularly blinking'.

Here's an example of letting your fears fuel something larger. It's from 'He Said' by 2014 Australian Poetry Slam champion Zohab Zee Khan.

MY FIRST TIME (CHICAGO)

My first time. I was 19 and snuck into the Green Mill bar where Marc Smith has been hosting poetry slams since 1986.

I can't remember if I lied about my age or if Marc just said, 'No drinking – but come and jump into our open mic.' (In the States, you have to be 21 to go into bars.)

I made a huge mess of it.

First of all, I performed a theatre monologue I'd performed for my school's end-of-year recital. It was in the voice of a teenaged English punk who couldn't stand boring people on the bus, which included me ripping open my bag and shouting, 'Think something. Do something.' And other such things. Anyway I went ages over time and no one liked it. They were telling me to get off the stage.

But I kept going. I tried other spoken word nights. I formed a band, writing lyrics, shouting them over drums, bass and guitar. By the time I moved to Australia, I knew I wanted to be a writer. All I had was a notebook full of lyrics and half-formed stories.

MILES

He said,
'Go back to where you came from,
YOU
DIRTY
TERRORIST!'
He called me,
A dirty terrorist.
But,
To be honest,
This isn't the first time I've heard this.
So I've become used to such abuse,
And I've learnt to pick and choose
what I listen to.
But this,
this was new.
This time,
This middle aged man,
Held in his hand,
The hand of his ten year old son.

Talk about your rollercoaster. You are not always the hero. Throw some underdog self-deprecation in there. Let the audience tell you how amazing you are. Sometimes – surprise – you aren't even in the piece. Your characters are. You do not always have to play yourself on stage. Think dialogue. Think gesture.

... and change minds (a little bit)

At the end of your performance, you want people feeling like: 'I may not agree with you on everything, but my view has shifted'. You do this through telling a story – not by simply expressing an opinion (open yawn). Like we said back in our discussion of metaphor (pages 40–44), when people hear opinions they get the opportunity to disagree, but when they hear a story they walk away with a warm fuzzy feeling, thinking how strange love is or asking themselves, 'Who will *I* be?'

Stories chip away at perceptions. Sometimes a member of your audience will have an epiphany, return home and invite their new neighbours over for dinner or never use plastic straws again or start their own creative democratic forum in their local library and call it a poetry slam.

Ten tricks to make your performance fly

Why tricks and not ideas? Um ... hello! You are a magician. This is your magic show. You are going to pull some cray-cray stuff out of your head. Expect the audience to flip out watching your dreams somersault across the stage. By now, if you've been putting this book down to go and try some of the exercises, you should have a draft poem or story that you are preparing to perform for friends or to an audience. You've poured your bubbling mix of heart and intellect into words. You've created a little paper plane of dream-life. Here's how you make it fly.

Trick 1: Movement

From the moment you are called up to perform, your audience is watching you. Your movements are part of your show.

You move with confidence directly to the microphone. Feet are spread just a touch wider than your shoulders. Shoulders are back. Hands are free. You breathe in. You breathe out. Centre yourself. Breathe in and ... speak. Boom! This is what I call the Standard Power Walk.

Or ... what happens if your name is called and, instead of going directly to the mic, you are seated in the audience? Your poem/story just begs for you to be one of the crowd.

You look around as the audience gets anxious waiting for you to fill the empty stage. You stand, pull the cordless mic from behind your back and speak. Hopefully you're in a venue with a follow spot (a spotlight that can be moved to follow you), the house lights are up or the lighting person is in on the trick so they have a special spot set up for you. You still want to be seen. You can make your way to the stage while you perform, or you can stay in the audience. Step around them. Stand on a chair. This is the ultimate we-are-all-passengers-on-the-same-bus opener.

TRY THIS

MIME IT

Find three spots in one of your written poems where you can add a snippet of mime (it's okay, you can speak as you move) or insert a gesture. Then practise a variety of entrances, starting with the Standard Power Walk described above.

How about you slide, commando style, across the stage? Do a forward roll? Run, skip? Rip open your yellow raincoat ... You see where this is going?

You might not get the cool lighting guy, or the cordless mic, or the follow spot. Assess the room, figure out what will surprise the crowd *and* fit the context of your poem. Then ... Your name is called ... and ENTRANCE – the big movement that kicks off your stage time.

This is a show. You are the sole character and performer. How will you fill this space? It has to be with more than just words. So movement, at minimum, will be the Standard Power Walk entrance combined with gesture. Those hands have to move with purpose and intention. You punctuate your points with action. You grab onto the reins and gallop as you describe your first horse ride. Move your hand slowly up your body and above your head, and pop your hand open like a sunflower as you sing about your luscious garden.

Emotional hand waving or throwing your arms wide is okay for a bit of emphasis but the good stuff is planned, choreographed and meaningful. Pull back the bow. Flip through the pages. Yes, okay, it may look like amateur mime sometimes, but people are listening, following the pictures and actions you are painting with words. You will add to the impact of your imagery with conscious gestures.

Trick 2: Sound effects

Your performance on stage is anything you can do with mouth and body. Right? This means you can sing, scream, whistle, stutter, go for a whole lot of onomatopoeia – *bang, zoom, vroom* – and experiment. Add vocal sound effects.

CRAFTING THE SOUND

'Good spoken word poetry utilises aural tools to make it sound a specific way. The use of alliteration, rhyme, onomatopoeia, repetition, tone and speed of delivery makes it particularly beautiful and interesting to listen to.'

Candy Royalle,
poet and activist

PLAYING WITH PITCH

'I put in a lot of thought about tone and harmony. I guess when I perform spoken word, even though I'm not a musician, a lot of the time my words have a pitch!'

Maxine Beneba Clarke,
writer and spoken word poet

Also think about the loud and soft bits. This is called **modulation,** and it helps to emphasise your emotions. We all know that if someone shouts in a conversation they're excited or angry – or the music is too loud. It means something. What could a whisper mean? Try long pauses. Why write 'I laugh' when you can just laugh? You can add all kinds of emotional interjections. Instead of saying 'He picks up the glass', just reach your hand out, grab the glass and guzzle.

Pitch refers to high and low notes – in music, or just in your speaking voice.

Please don't finish every sentence on a higher note. Read these two sentences out loud:

Your statements sound like questions.
Your statements sound like questions?

LOOP PEDALS

Get into some advanced-level audio experimentation by plugging your mic into a loop pedal. Tap the pedal to record sounds live. Tap it again and what you've recorded begins playing repeatedly in a loop.

With a loop pedal you can lay down your own rhythm section by layering pops, clicks, melodies and beatboxing sounds until you have a soundtrack you're happy with. The music you've created will keep playing while you speak along with it. Content is still queen/king. But once you feel confident in that department this tech play is heaps o' fun. Play with it for a long time and watch some YouTube tutorials before trying in front of a crowd.

I've used this to create soundscapes, like layering several bird calls until the venue sounds like an aviary full of kookaburras, cockatoos and whistling warblers. Look up US comedian/musician Reggie Watts for some excellent examples of this technique.

Your statements, if you want them to resonate with confidence, should end on the same note as the rest of the words in the sentence, or on a lower note.

Of course you can play with this. A child-like voice is often represented as high; an old man's voice, or a serious voice, is deep. Play with these notions. Find the musicality in your sentences.

You have this mad gamut of movement and sound available to you, so use it to bend expectations. The tricky thing here is maintaining an emotional connection with your audience. Ensure each tick and click is in context. People will be impressed if you walk on stage on your hands while belting an operatic aria into the mic, then deliver a poem completely unrelated to acrobatics and song. But they'll see the opener as a trick unrelated to your work. You'd be better off advancing the story or the arc of your writing. Think of it like this: you're watching a 3D film, and suddenly there's a scene in an asteroid field. You just know the director threw it in to make you duck, because it didn't fit the rest of the script. Heart rate up, yes. But it's a cheap trick – let's get back to the hero's impending doom.

Sound, pitch and movement: use them in line with your purpose.

Trick 3: Speed

This is where you chooosssse to eeeelongaaate a liiine as you move your body like a robot running low on battery power. It's the slow-mo setting as you lean back, lift one foot off the floor and stick your boot up your racist boss's bum. It's also the super-quick race to the finish line.

This is where you get to put rhythm into practice. You throw in some rhymes and speak to a fast beat:

> Rain is seventeen year
> Cicada plague
> Ga-ga-ga-gone kamikaze
> On my nylon A-frame.
> A Ballina hurricane
> spins in my racing brain.

Speaking quickly can also represent anxiety. If it's done as a clear character, it's great. But your audience might also hear this as your own anxiety. You are going to be full of adrenaline, which will cause you to speed up. You'll have to consciously slow down, add pauses, and articulate and clearly pronounce each word. You might think you're speaking too slowly but your audience will hear a normal conversational pace.

You want to articulate and pronounce each word. This relates closely to what we talked about with using concrete language (page 31) – you've only got 2 or 3 minutes on stage. You have to tell a story with imagery and action instead of abstract language or your audience will tune out. Likewise, if your audience is missing lines because you're rattling them off too quickly, they will stop listening. They may pick up a couple of key words, get the gist and applaud, but they'll miss your message.

You have no replay button in a live event. Words wash

> **WARM UP AND WHISPER**
>
> **TRY THIS**
>
> Warm up your vocals by humming scales. Stretch your lips and jaw open as wide as you can. Then clearly speak all the vowels.
>
> If you are going to whisper in your poem, practise something called a *sotto voce*. This is Latin for 'under the voice' or 'beneath the voice'. In a poem, this can be loud but with a lot of breath. Try speaking a line in a loud whisper. Lowering your voice can create emphasis or drama, as though the thing you're saying is meant to shock.

into our ears and clear the way for the next wave of syllables. Give them time to be processed. On a recording, or in a song you sing at every concert, people will give you their ear more readily for sped-up language while they mine your verses for meaning. But in a live spoken word setting, too fast just means tuned out. There is no music to carry the audience through your flood. There is no rewinding and playing again. You have to remember people are there to hear your content, not your beat. They haven't read your book yet so they're not reciting along with you.

Imagine a track with the sickest beat. One that makes you wanna jump, bump and shake that thang. One that

DROP THE BEAT

I saw US Poetry Slam champion turned hip-hop artist Sage Francis perform in a Sydney venue called The Basement. In the middle of his set, music still flowing, he stopped and said something like: 'Look at you all. I could say anything. You would be bobbing your heads to this beat. I could tell you what gym shoes to buy. I can tell you who to vote for and you all wouldn't give a damn. You'd just be bobbing your heads to the beat. So listen up' – here he began rapping again, just repeating over and over – 'Dance monkey dance! Dance monkey dance!'

I was not dancing. I stopped when he started talking, but all those dudes with shoe brands on their baseball caps and T-shirts were bouncing, jumping and singing along. Lesson: your words are more important than your beats.

MILES

DON'T THROW IT AWAY

'I wish spoken word poets would stop throwing away the last line of their poems, like mumbling them, or kind of getting off stage before they've even said it. The last line is like the most important line of the whole damn thing. Give it the time it deserves.'

Luka Lesson, spoken word poet, hip-hop artist, educator and 2011 Australian Poetry Slam Champion

makes you want to celebrate. But wait – what are those lyrics? 'Hey hey hey / Uranium mining should be done by kids / Cos you don't have pay pay pay / Oh yeah! Buy my toothpaste – it's the best!' (Repeat × 5.)

Better stick with the instrumental version, hey?

The combo of great message and superb bounce is ideal but the message is *always* paramount. Give them stiff gulps, solid sips and bone-shivering shots. Don't just break the levee on them with an overwhelming flow. Well, yeah, do that – but do it while enunciating each word in an onslaught of nouns, verbs, sounds and movement, leading to a climactic crescendo:

He uses two names.
Calls himself something cold

Like a train braking
Like a tone
TV tone
Telling you, WAKE UP! Show's over.
[*Long, high-pitched nasal hum into
    microphone*]
But you want to know his real name?
[*Ask the audience until they respond with
    'YES!' Then, while slowly extending your
    right arm out in front of you, opening your
    fist and reaching out to the audience, release
    these words in a long raspy breath*:]
Sssaaaaaave meeeeeee.

TRY THIS

PACE YOURSELF

Experiment with speed. Pick a section of your
own text to say really quickly or slow right down.
Test out speaking your words to a beat. Find an
instrumental track and speak to the rhythm of the
track. Also choose a section to go super slo-mo –
include slowed-down movements as well. It's you
at half-speed.

REFLECT, CONNECT

'When you're on stage it's not about you. It's about standing with a massive mirror. It's me trying to connect with that audience. If they can see a little bit of themselves in this six foot six, moustached brown man, that's me done for the day, that's me done for life.'

Zohab Zee Khan, author, educator and 2014 Australian Poetry Slam Champion

Trick 4: Audience interaction

Eye contact with the audience is the minimum level of interaction to aim for. You can't do this with every person in the room but you can pick out people and deliver your lines directly to them. In larger venues I imagine the audience is in the form of a clock laid flat. To my right is 3 o'clock. In the middle is 12 o'clock. On my left is 9 o'clock. I pick a person at each point on the clock and make a connection with them. I don't turn my head in an obvious arch of nods. I just ensure that I give attention in all directions.

Making eye contact and speaking to a particular person will add immediacy and intimacy to your performance. You are not performing to the lights or the back wall. You are not presenting to a group. You are chatting with a few people in a semi-circle while everyone

MAKE THE AUDIENCE WORK

TRY THIS

Find a section in your poem where you can speak directly to the audience. Think of a task you can give to one person or all of the crowd. Write in the instructions as notes to yourself. If you're publishing this work as well, you can keep the notes out. But, for example, just remember on these lines you will say 'Poet', and the crowd will respond with 'Tree'.

listens in. You are not in your head having an out-of-body experience, losing yourself in the poem. You are here with the people who care. They care enough to put away whatever they were going to do with their time. They choose to give their time (and in many cases their money) to you. Look at them. Give them a gift. Ask them questions. Engage them. Walk off stage and sit with one of them for a brief moment. Stay on mic, though, so everybody can hear.

Give your audience some actions. I finish one poem by getting the audience to make popping sounds with their lips to mimic rain drops. In longer performances, I might raise my hand and ask, 'Who's been camping before? In the rain? In a thunderstorm? When your tent gets lifted off the ground while you're in it?' There's usually at least one person left with their hand in the air. I either walk to them with the mic or invite them on stage and interview them about their experience. If you have the chance to perform a longer solo show, remember that a direct human-to-human interaction is a powerful addition.

Trick 5: The solo script

By now, you probably have the makings of a one-person script of 2–3 minutes. You've imagined the room with the audience in it. Now, in addition to the words you will say, create notes for yourself next to the text. Like:

Sound FX – Insert pigeon cooing sound here

Blocking – Point right finger up and spin on one foot

Volume – Get loud here / Whisper this word

Speed – Rapid fire delivery / Long pause

OFF SCRIPT

Charlie Chaplin did not use scripts for his early silent films. He wrote a list of actions. Once they were filmed, the list was no longer necessary. Crumple. Bin.

Because you are going to commit this piece of writing to memory, your script will not be necessary for very long. You will embody all of the directions you've written down. But this text will be a reference if you ever decide you'd like others to perform your writing.

You can also consider using the text for publication online or in print. (Spoken word poems are usually published without the notes, but if they work as part of the reader's experience, try publishing with stage notes.) But your best document is video, capturing both the words and the performance.

You probably have access to a recording device on your phone or someone else's. Use it often. Create an audio journal. Turn the camera around and video yourself, performing your poetry. It's gonna feel weird and you're going to be hypercritical those first couple of

THEY LISTEN

'I just loved how [at a poetry slam] the audience listened so closely to every word. Of course, I love hip-hop gigs, but often times it's about vibe and energy, and the words you have worked so hard on get lost in the mix.'

Omar Musa, spoken word poet and hip-hop artist

RECORD IT – DIRECT IT

TRY THIS

There are three tasks here.

1   Recite the poem you've been writing along with this book and record it onto your device. Listen back. See if there are edits you can make based on how it sounds. How long is your performance?
2   Spend at least a week doing mini–audio journal entries. Any ideas that pop into your head, record them.
3   Find a spoken word artist whose work you like and ask them if they can give you feedback. Schedule a time when you can perform your poem for them and listen to their directions. This can be as formal or casual as you choose. I would aim for the formal. Like find a rehearsal space in a local hall or library and really take it seriously. Consider offering to pay them as a director, mentor or coach.

times you see yourself onscreen. Keep studying your presentation, though. Look at the expressions on your face, your movements, your articulation, your volume and pace. Show it to a couple of others or, better still, try a live version in front of a couple of friends. Performance is a great editor. You will instantly recognise when a word feels out of place. In particular, the live experience allows you to see how people react to lines, giving you a general sense as to whether the writing is working.

But Australian spoken word audiences are generous. They will applaud you for giving it a go: 'So brave. You expressed yourself in front of us. So cool.' Clap clap clap. So this is a good start, but it's not always a reliable editing tool. In comedy, it's easy to know if something works. The crowd laughs? Good. The crowd stays silent and claps at the end? Not good. Spoken word isn't quite like that, so it's necessary, as you grow artistically, to seek feedback on your work from a professional artist who can help you edit your writing and direct your performance. If you have someone giving you feedback or can hire someone – like a mentor, coach, director or editor – your work will get stronger. In Australia there is no formal industry around performed writing ... yet. In the meantime, peers, colleagues and mentors are the oil on the grinding wheel helping us sharpen our gifts.

Trick 6: Practise, rehearse, memorise

Take the text you have written. Say it out loud to yourself several times. Record it. Listen or watch. Keep it playing on loop in the background as you do the dishes, sit on the bus, drive around town ... even when you sleep.

Maxine Beneba Clarke spoke about her process of memorising, and how it's changed over the years. 'When I first started writing pieces that I knew were going to be performed, I wasn't writing them down. So I'd go for a walk around the neighbourhood or whatever. I'd get the first line right. Memorise it over and over. Then I'd go into the second line. That was how I was writing pieces – not putting them down on paper.'

Her process changed when she had enough poems – about 20 – to publish a book, so she had to get them into written form. 'So now I don't do it in my head', she says. 'I'll always write it on a whiteboard or a piece of paper or whatever, but I will say each line out loud. So before I write line three, I've already spoken lines one and two a few times and worked out what that means.'

My process is different. For memorising writing I generally use rote. I simply begin saying the piece without looking at the page. When I make a mistake, I have a peek at the correct line. I say the line three times slowly, then look away and start from the beginning. I do this until I can recite the entire piece.

There is whole school of memorisation techniques known as **mnemonics**. One of the most common mnemonic tools using is **associative imagery**. The images must be graphic, they must be wild, and they must be born out of the thing you are memorising (see box, page 106).

Another mnemonic technique is to create an acronym sentence. 'Every Good Boy Deserves Favour' is a way to remember the musical notes on the lines of the treble clef, from bottom to top.

You're in luck if your writing does use rhythm and rhyme. Making a poem is a memorisation tool in itself. When I'm struggling with a screwdriver, trying to twist

ASSOCIATIVE IMAGERY

Here's an example. I'm on a tour bus with my mum on Fraser Island, and the tour guide points to a tree and says, 'That's a turpentine. Latin name *sincarpia*. And the big green plant stuck to the side is an epiphyte.'

I want to memorise these random facts.

I imagine a large, half-naked carp smoking a cigar and wearing a boxer's robe. It's swinging and grumbling through a cheering melee toward a spot-lit boxing ring. The carp drinks from a huge brown bottle marked 'turpentine'.

An *epic fight* for a *sinful carp* drinking *turps*.

An epiphyte on a sincarpia or turpentine tree.

MILES

this little head of metal, I say to myself, 'Tighty righty, lefty loosey'. Kids repeat this line to each other: 'You get what you get and you don't get upset.'

Narrative is also an excellent form for memorisation. It's often used to reinforce or remember behaviour.

Know your pieces so well that you can sit inside of them. Move around in them. Be sure that when you face an audience you can adapt to the room. You need to be there with the audience, not busily trying to recall a word or line. Your relationship with the audience is stronger if you can respond to the specific circumstances in front

TRY THIS

SPEAK WITHOUT TEXT

Memorise it! Here is where you use all of the above memorisation techniques until you find one that's right for you. Memorise up to 3 minutes of poetry to start with. As you write new material, memorise it. You will need a quiet space to yourself. Also use your recording – play, listen, stop, recite, and extend the amount you can recite each time you stop the recording. Think of some banter – anecdotes and engaging stories that can introduce your poems and put you on course to have a full set. You're working toward a suite of poems – about five or six of varying lengths, with enough conversation in between to cover 20 minutes.

of you and improvise around the text. If you show up to the event to see that half the audience is kids and the other half is their grandparents, you should be prepared to change any swear words to zoo animals. I have about 3 hours of poems, stories, lyrics and monologues in my head. I can do a 50-minute primary school show, a 2-hour adult show or almost anything in between. I've got my handy portable repertoire in my head.

If you are going to pursue the whole dream of performing your writing, then you are not only writing for yourself. You're writing for a variety of audiences.

Trick 7: Get out there

Start going to spoken word events in bookshops, cafés, music venues, art centres, community halls everywhere. Watch a bunch of poetry slam videos and stand-up comedy. Observe how the performers move their bodies, how they move the microphone, how they interact with audiences. Do your research. Watching live shows will be powerful and informative. (Because this book is in print, and spoken word events can be ephemeral, we've created a *Slam Your Poetry* page on www.australianpoetryslam. com to keep you up to date with the latest links to gigs and organisations.)

In this scoping out of local events, you'll find your tribe. The community where you feel most at home. The right atmosphere. The organiser will have a clear sign-up process, which will usually be a piece of paper near the front door. Otherwise walk up to one of the organisers

TRY THIS

YOU MUST MEET PEOPLE

Put this book back into your little shoulder satchel or backpack, add your notebook and grab your water bottle. Make sure the lid is on tight and it's stored in an outside pocket. Don't want to get your stuff wet. Now go. Get out of the house. Check out a slam or open mic. Sit and watch. Mingle. Get comfortable. Go a couple of times. Then, when you're ready ... sign up and perform. The first few times you perform, bring that notebook or notes app on your phone on stage with you. Read from it but be sure to look up and make eye contact after every few lines. Bring water on stage with you. Take a gulp beforehand. If you've got time and a couple of poems, take regular sips from your water. Either get a glass from the venue or ... hey, you brought some with you – awesome!

and ask if you can perform. Try an open mic or a slam. Open mics might give you 5 minutes. Slams give you 2–3 minutes. That's all you have to do – get 2 minutes of your ideas together and you will be able to find an audience. Your longer term aim is to have a solid 20-minute show, which could be a collection of your short pieces with some banter and anecdotes thrown in.

Open mics and slams won't pay you. If you win a slam there will be a pay-off – ultimately you want a feature spot and you want to get paid. But this will not cover your bills if you're just starting out. The opportunities for making a good living just aren't there yet. I'd guess that around 200 people in Australia work as performing writers part-time or full-time through a mix of paid performances, teaching, producing spoken word projects and events, grants, advertising work and merchandise.

The real value is in the sharing. While you'll have listeners, you are also there to support other people in the community and be a listener yourself. That is part of the exchange in slam or open mic. It's mutual sharing. Sometimes you'll be an audience member cheering and sometimes you'll be on stage.

Trick 8: Breathing and stage fright

Take deep breaths. Breathe in through your nose, out through your mouth. As you inhale, push your abdomen out so it feels like you're filling your tummy with air. If your shoulders are rising, then change it up.

Why? You can fit more air in when you breathe from your diaphragm, which means you can speak for longer without inhaling. It also means you can project your voice with more power. This is what actors and singers do. They train themselves to breathe using the diaphragm. You are an artist too. This is part of your craft.

Close your eyes. Focus on the air flowing over your upper lip as you inhale and exhale. Observe any sensations – tickling, itching, heat or cold – in that triangle of nose and mouth. Don't react. Just observe.

If you're doing this, you're meditating. This will also help to relieve stress before, during and after a gig.

Yawn to relax your throat. Take quick drinks of warm water, but don't drink anything with caffeine in it.

Remember that you can joke about your nervousness. If you choose to be vulnerable, your audience will understand.

TRY THIS

BREATHE

Hey, you're off the hook – trick number 8 is an exercise in itself. The only extra thing I'd suggest is checking out a couple of YouTube clips on breathing from your diaphragm.

Trick 9: Shake it out

Your body before a performance will be full of adrenaline. Your heart will be thumping. You will be scared while you wait to go on stage. If you're featuring in an event, you should find a backstage area. Go there. Shake your arms. Jump in place. If I've got a whole lot of space I do a few laps.

You don't want to use up all of your adrenaline but think of it like this: we are animals. Animals get this same hit of adrenaline when they face a predator. This hormonal rush is really valuable in the wild where the roo, gazelle or mouse must run for its life or turn and fight. Both of these physically draining actions use up the juice squeezed from adrenal glands. We experience the same kick but sit at a desk or stand frozen at the mic. Perhaps we are representing the third position animals take when a threat is near: standing super-still, pretending we're statues or playing dead. Instead, get your circulation going. Get your body to match your anxiety level.

When you get on stage, turn your shaking hands into precise gestures. Shaking hands are obvious when you're holding paper or a device, so keep your hands free. Cut through the fear by being larger than life or incredibly focused and precise. Use fear to fuel your onstage power. Choreograph your movements.

Your anxiety will be short-lived if you have rehearsed. Once you begin speaking, and you have the audience's attention and hear them responding, you'll be able to just have a chat with them.

Imagine this. An incredible thing has just happened. You're racing to meet your friend at the café. You perch on a seat and let loose this incredible story to your friend. You know the story, and all the points that lead to the climactic result. You're excited and animated, not getting bogged down in extra words. You churn out talk like an espresso-fuelled engine. Your friend is excited now, elated. At the end of your revelation, your friend breathes a 'Phew! That's amazing.' At no point is your friend thinking, 'This sounds rehearsed. What is she

TRY THIS

BREAK THE POETRY RHYTHM

Record yourself speaking your poem. Listen back. Try it again but really just speak it as though it's a chat. It's your normal voice. You're not emphasising the end of a line. Not picking up the rhymes and making a spoken beat. Just talking your poem like a good anecdote.

talking about?' No – you're just you talking to a friend with all the passion that bubbles up through your experience of the world.

This mix of passion, excitement and conversation is what you bring to the stage. Yes you will have angry poems, and you will have sad poems, but always say to yourself: *The audience is my friend. I've raced here to see my friend and this is what I have to tell them.*

Trick 10: Using the mic

The mic is your best mate. Usually the mic is the only thing you share the stage with. If you don't know how to work with it, things ain't gonna go well. You might hear someone say from the back of the room 'Speak-up!' or 'Stand closer to the mic! We can't hear you.'

Or, worse, you might catch a look of disdain and hands over ears as the mic distorts because you're shouting into it, or there's feedback (loud, high-pitched, ear-splitting sounds) because you're pointing the mic at that big audio speaker thingy over your shoulder.

If you can afford it, buy a mic and a little amp. Practise at home. I mean, think about it. If you were gonna learn to play the bass or electric guitar, you'd go out and get the gear, right?

Those of us who regularly perform our writing can usually just rock up to a venue and get straight into the available audio. No problem. Speak here. Look at audience. Done. Right? The people who make mic technique look easy have either been on stage a lot or they have their own mini-kit at home.

There's no need to invest in audio toys straightaway. Just know the places you perform will all have slightly different microphone set-ups.

If you've got a choice, go for a cordless radio mic on a straight stand. This gives you the most range. You can take the mic off the stand and rove; you can lean forward when you whisper and lean back when you're loud. When the mic's on the stand, you can move your hands around if you want to. Or if you plan to keep the mic in your hand in the whole time, you can pick the stand up and move it out of the spotlight. No need to clutter the space with unnecessary gear. But you might dance with the stand, pretend to lean on it or use it for air-jousting (actually I've never done that and wouldn't really recommend it). Just pop the mic back into the stand when you need both your hands.

A straight stand is your best bet. The boom stand –

the kind that has a couple of poles and can bend – takes up too much space and is only relevant if you are playing an instrument seated, or if the mic needs quick adjusting for other performers who may take the stage before or after you. A boom stand can be tilted back easily. A straight stand will either have a squeeze trigger handle to allow you to move it up and down, or will have a twistable ring. Remember: righty tighty, lefty loosey.

You might not get a choice of mics. If it's a mic with a cable, just be aware of what the cable's doing. If you choose to walk or pace the stage, like a stand-up comedian, then unwind the cable from the stand. Sound engineers usually wind the cable in a spiral around the stand. You can do exactly the same things with a cable mic as you do with a cordless. You're just more restricted in your movement.

The ideal spot for holding a mic is just below your chin, so all of your 'p', 't' and 'k' sounds don't distort and pop into the mic. If you shout, pull the mic away from your mouth. Pull the mic in close for a whisper.

You do not need to eat the mic. Move it away from your mouth. Whoever is looking after the sound should be able to set the mic levels so that you don't have to shove it between your lips. The only time this is appropriate mic behaviour is when you work with music and your voice has to compete with drums and guitars ... or if you're beatboxing or trying to impersonate a dragon for the little ones down the front. (Raaaar!)

Also, if you hold the mic in front of your mouth, it obscures your face from the audience, the photographer and anyone video-recording the performance. Keep it below the chin.

Here are a couple more mic etiquette bits.

- Don't drop the mic. It's not yours. It can break. I know you've heard about mic drops. Event organisers hate them. Respect the mic. All hail the mighty mic.
- I've seen people walk away from the mic for effect. 'I want to go a cappella', they say, barefoot on stage. 'I just want to be natural. I'm anti-technology.' That's cool, but nobody at the back of the room can hear you. Often gigs are recorded, then broadcast on radio, podcast, YouTube. No mic = no recording.
- Watch out for headset mics. You can't move them back and forth and all around. Your vocal modulation and range are set and at the mercy of the sound engineer. Engineers in professional venues are really good, but if your performance goes from a whisper to a shout and back again, the engineer will have to be prepared to lower and increase your volume on the fly – unless they have a script with your notes, or you've been able to have a comprehensive sound check. If you have to use a headset because it's a conference and that's all they got, then be ready to adapt.
- Check the mic sound to make sure it's at the right level. If you are in a large space, ask for foldback speakers. These are speakers that face you, allowing you to hear your volume.

Ensemble performances and teams

Here's that group poem talk we've been saying is coming. These can be hella powerful. The messages are reinforced and the layering of sound is mesmerising and sometimes uplifting. The US National Poetry Slam, Canadian Slam and slams in many countries have the team category or two different slam competitions. In Australia, the slams that do regular team events are Bankstown Poetry Slam's grand final, OutLoud youth slam in Victoria and Slamalamadingdong in Melbourne.

There are many ways to divide a poem or a piece of writing into multiple voices.

1   One person writes a poem, then breaks up the poem into parts and delegates those parts to others, or gets collaborators to pick parts that 'speak' to them.

2   Each writer contributes a stanza on a topic, or four lines, or however many lines each person wants to contribute.

3   The group passes a piece of paper around in a circle as poets finish each other's sentences or respond to the sentence before.

4   The group just records an intense conversation, edits it down and re-enacts the conversation. This merges with **verbatim theatre**, where the recording plays in the ear of the performer as they take on the voices of the people speaking in their headphones. Try a duet, trio or quartet or more.

We were sitting on the floor watching bands in an underground club called The Goodbar in Paddington, inner Sydney. The MC came on in between acts and said that there'd be a 10-minute open mic for anyone in the room.

My partner nudged me. 'Why don't you get up and just read something from your notebook?' I waited for a bit to see if anyone else was going to get up. She pushed me again: 'Go on.'

I stood up and walked through the crowd. The sound system was pumping out something loud. The MC asked me, off-mic, 'What are you gonna do?'

'I'm gonna do a poem.'

'A poem? Listen, it's kind of a band night,' he said. 'It's not really the right fit.'

Nobody else came forward, so I asked if I could just give it a try anyway.

'Alright, okay, okay', he shrugged, turning to the mic. 'Hey everybody! We've got ... what's your name? Miles. Miles the poet.'

He pointed to me and said, 'Five minutes max.'

I got up on stage. They turned off the pumping dance track. The crowd was milling and mumbling. With my notebook shaking in my hands and the spotlight blinding me, I belted out a poem about a cute couple who burn down cities in America. I was nervous but covered it up with acting skills that made me sound confident.

After a couple of stanzas the packed club was silent. I kept going. Speeding up, slowing down. Throwing onomatopoeia into the mic. Using the voices of two different characters. Finding rhythm and stopping it mid-flow. Whispering. Singing. Hitting the verbs hard. Working myself up into a frenzy of anger and laughter. Until I hit my final line ... *Kidnapping people like you.*

The audience was still silent. I waited, unsure. Then I realised they were waiting, expecting me to say more. I heard someone toward the back of the club say, 'Wow.'

I timidly asked, 'Do you want to hear another one?'

'Yeah!' they actually roared.

I got the biggest hit of endorphins, adrenaline, whatever joy hormones fill a person's brain and face to make them smile and blush at the same time. It felt sooo good. Nerdy black kid. Not sitting anonymously, invisibly, in a crowd.

When my time was up I walked off stage. A woman asked me if I could perform at a gallery a few days later. That's how I got offered my first paid gig.

I started creating scripts for my own solo performances in pubs, cafés, bookshops and little theatre spaces. I performed poetry, stories, monologues and lyrics, and experimented with vocal and electronic sound effects. And all the time I kept pushing the definitions of poetry.

The rush of performing is great. The opportunity to skip a barista shift and perform some poems for pay? Well, I began stringing enough gigs together to quit the café!

MILES

Once the poem is written, you can then use a system like underlining the words you will say together, circling words you will echo, and adding in some synchronised movements and vocal sound effects.

You can also create dialogues and multi-voice conversations. Hey, wait a minute – isn't that just a play? Oh yeah! Do we need silos that break creative self-expression up into labels, categories, genres, definitions, communities and forms? I think not. A song can be dialogue written and peformed a cappella in a poetry event with projections and live drawing. Podcasts, stand-up comedy, audiobooks ... these are all forms of performed writing. So don't limit yourself to just the 2-minute poem.

Keep your instrument tuned

Now I know at this point that some of you are like, 'I just want free expression. I don't care about all this practise/memorise/study stuff. It's crushing my flow.'

But think about why you're doing this. Is it just to have some fun at the local open mic or slam? If it is, that's cool. It may be that it just feels damn good to shout what you feel to a cheering crowd of new friends. Or get your words in front of you so you can heal from the break-up or celebrate the graduation.

I am advocating for all of the above. Poetry and performance should just be part of everyday normal life. You can take all the performance suggestions seriously or you can dip in and out, taking on a few hints here and there and leaving others. With this book, we want to put all options on the table, so if you decide to pursue a career as a performing writer, the option will eventually be open. It will take hard work and perseverance. A cello player doesn't just pick up a bow to make the magic sounds start flowing. Your words, voice and body are the cello and bow. Learn how to tune yourself and pour out poems.

Then go out and find a stage ...

4

GET GIGS

We're not going to list a whole bunch of gigs in this book. You can have a look at the list of links (page 296) at the end, though – the info on those web pages will totally be much more up to date than this piece of paper.

In a poetry slam you have no props, costumes or instruments. But after you participate in a couple of poetry slams as a springboard for your work, you should be aiming for a minimum 20-minute show with a mix of poem lengths, from 1 minute to 8 minutes. The length is really up to you. I've performed 20-minute poems made up of several scenes revolving around a theme. Winners of the national Australian Poetry Slam receive an international tour to writers' festivals. This can mean an hour-long, one-person show in a bookshop in Beijing, so three 2-minute poems are not going to be enough. Sure, you will become a ninja poet, able to aim for the jugular and the gut, and get the standing ovation in 1 minute 45 seconds. But once you've been catapulted into the spotlight, you'll need a full repertoire to propel you further. Start building poems now.

AUSTRALIAN POETRY SLAM SUCCESS STORIES

Winning the Australian Poetry Slam has led to the successful careers of performing writers like Omar Musa (2008), Luka Lesson (2011), Zohab Zee Khan (2014), Solli Raphael (2017) and Melanie Mununggurr-Williams (2018).

Omar Musa went on to make several albums; publish a novel that was longlisted for the Miles Franklin Award, Australia's most prestigious literary prize; and has toured his own work steadily ever since.

Luka Lesson tours his shows to festivals and schools internationally, produces albums and publishes his work.

Solli Raphael was crowned the APS Youth Champion in 2017 at the age of 12. He went on to close the 2018 Commonwealth Games with a poem, deliver a TEDxSydney talk, publish a book, and work with Greenpeace and World Vision.

Melanie Munungurr-Williams, from north-east Arnhem Land, is one of 4600 speakers of the Yolŋu Matha languages. After her performance at the national final, she was offered a book deal, a 7-week tour of Canada and dozens of shows across the Asia-Pacific region.

A couple of general things to consider. In slams and in open mics, your time is your total time on stage. No long introductions. No preambles in addition to the poems. In a longer set you can tell a few poignant stories. I've seen these legends of folk music at festivals and they all have 'I'm tuning my guitar' stories. They might do a 45-minute set and only sing five songs. The rest of the time they've got the rehearsed story banter going on.

Don't apologise for your work or be self-deprecating. You will stuff up. Keep going. If you fall, turn it into a forward roll and say, 'Ta da!' The audience doesn't know what's on your paper, on your phone screen or in your head. Maybe the poem *does* have a line that repeats three times, getting louder each time. (No one knows it's because you forgot a line.) Go all impro. Go freestyle.

Types of events and artists

Here are the options for performing your poetry for a live audience as this book is being written.

Open mic

These are the most accessible type of event if you're just starting out. They can be found in almost every capital city in the world and many regional centres. Most are just 'turn up and sign up'; some will have a sign-up form in the comments section of their online promo; some have a mix of pre-registration and at-the-door sign-ups. The event may be exclusively for poetry, or open to a

DEEP LISTENING

'Before and after you get up, take the time to listen to others. Open mics are an exchange of performing and listening. You'll learn from others but also just appreciate the work of others. If you want people to take the time to listen to you, you owe them the same courtesy so leave time to stay for at least most of the event and don't leave once you had your turn.'

Benjamin Solah, poet and Director of Melbourne Spoken Word

mixed bag of musicians, poets, stand-up comedians and everyone else besides. Occasionally they are themed or lightly curated by a host.

Open mics are usually a safe space to try out your new stuff. The crowds are supportive. A lot of audience members are there to watch a friend. The main potential pitfall of this is that the audience might not be engaged. The quality of the performances can range from super-dull to pretty awesome to indecipherable shouting into the mic to poignant heartfelt to waaay too long. The key here is listen to other poets. Show up early. Figure out the parameters – time limit, theme. Respect the organiser, the other poets and the space.

There are time limits, though. They usually start at 5 minutes or one piece – whichever is shorter – but they blow out to 15 or 20 minutes per random act. If you just want to try your stuff out, this is your ground zero – so invite your friends and give it a go.

Poetry slam

[Variations include Band Slam, Story Slam, Pitch Slam, Multilingual Slam. The 'slam' word just adds a competitive element to whatever your presentation theme is.]

On pages 1–6 we talked a bit about the slam form, but here's a recap. Poetry slams and story slams are very similar to open mics. Every Australian capital city has at least one, and some regional centres have their own slam competitions.

THE MOTH

The Moth is a storytelling organisation that presents theme-based storytelling events across the US and in various countries, including Australia. It's true stories told from the teller's own experience. They do it in slam style or in a series of features. They've got an awesome podcast and have spots on ABC Radio National. They run all kinds of workshops and education outreach stuff.

Anyone can sign up and do whatever they want on the mic but there are a few poetry slam rules, which are usually published alongside the event's promotional blurbage. Here are some usual ones:

1 Performers get 2 minutes on the mic. (Your time starts from your first word or when the timekeeper feels your performance has begun – I'm looking at you, mimes.) Points are deducted for going over time.
2 The performance and writing must be your own original work – no plagiarism or covers.
3 No props, costumes or music. Just you and the mic.
4 The work must have been written within the last 12 months. You can't roll out the same championship poem every year.
5 Judges are chosen randomly from the audience.
6 Judges score on a 0–10 scale. After each performance they hold up score cards. The highest and lowest scores are dropped, and the remaining scores added up.
7 The highest scoring performer gets a prize.

Ultimately a poetry slam is an open mic with judges ... unless you win it. If you win a local slam, you might get cash. You could also get a toy, a bottle of wine, a book, a gift certificate, a hug and/or an invitation to the next round.

For the slams that include rounds, there is a chance to win a final round, and if it's a national slam that could

ENCOURAGING COMMUNITIES

'The communities that are built around slams, particularly those that run regularly, are what really engage people ... the immediate feedback and encouragement was the thing that made me want to keep writing and performing. Those audiences and communities are always so warm.'

Emily Crocker, poet and the
Rumble Youth Slam Champion

mean touring, a book deal, paid gigs and potentially a career.

The good thing about slams is they're usually a touch more professional than the open mics. Because they're run as competitions, and judges are chosen from the audience, slams attract larger crowds than open mics.

The organisers often take photos, video or audio-record their events. They may even book you for other gigs.

The feature spot

en you've performed in a few open mics, won a couple
slams or made a cool recording of your work, you
ffered an opportunity to perform for pay. This

is known as the feature spot, and it's 10–30 minutes of you being on stage by yourself and wowing the audience.

Take all your poems and stories put 'em in a big pile and imagine you've been told: *We want to see your manuscript but it's got a maximum word count of 2500 words.* That's about 20 minutes of speaking. Which pieces will you choose and in what order? It's a bit like the process of making an album, or organising chapters in a novel.

Come in with a bang – a 30-second-or-less opener. I use a few, like:

> Hi, my name is Miles – not to be confused with kilometres, which are shorter and less imperial. Last name Merrill – like Merrill Lynch, but no financial expertise and no lynching please.

or …

> Good evening, crazies and mentalmen, and welcome to another edition of 'We're Not Normal'.

or (as mentioned previously) …

> [*A series of noises, beats, hums, coughs, snapping, high notes, throat-singing vibrato and hiccups that stop suddenly*] That was a poem called 'Some Things Cannot be Written Down'.

Come up with your own unique intro lines. Try them out.

Make people laugh. Surprise them. Enter by walking on your hands and say, 'This is me'.

Now you've got their attention, bring a 2-minute piece that gets them invested, then tell a story or perform a monologue. Whatever you do, show a diverse range.

You see this at poetry slam finals. Poet comes out, performs a stunner: '… and set them free!' Bows, gets mad applause. Round two is another stunner, but unfortunately it sounds exactly like the previous poem, just slightly different: '… if only we gave people their freedom!' Applause. Not mad applause. More of a hmm-that-was-really-good kind of applause. But people are thinking: *I get it. The words change but you keep saying the same thing.*

Variety! Change lengths, styles, forms, voices and movement. There are no official directors or coaches in Australia for spoken word poets. They do exist in the US, the UK and Europe. But in Australia, at the time of writing this, there are a few mentors trying to help out emerging artists. I recommend finding one. Most performing writers are using applause, slam scores, publication or number of video views to determine what works and what doesn't. That is not enough. If you are reading this book and doing the things I suggest, your work will stand out because no one else is getting clear direction.

So please – for my sake, for yours, for your audience's, for spoken word's sake – *change it up*. Yes, put in a comic bit. Yes, lie down on the floor. Yes, sing bits. Just change it up. Oh, and don't try to sound like someone else. Remember you can do whatever voice, body and

MIXING IT UP

'The most difficult aspect [of writing for performance] is trying to ensure each piece has its own feel, its own flow. It can sometimes be difficult not to produce pieces that sound too similar. I work hard on thinking of new ways to deliver work so that it's interesting for both the audience and myself, as well as honouring the piece itself in the way it should be honoured.'

Candy Royalle, poet and activist

mind allow, so why copy someone else? The whole point of the form is personal self-expression. This can be one of the drawbacks of slam competitions: people get afraid to experiment. They want to win. So they try to sound like the person who won the slam last year or someone they've seen on Button Poetry (a YouTube channel with millions of subscribers and hundreds of spoken word artist videos, mostly from American slams).

How to get a feature spot

If you've won a slam, the prize is often a short feature at the next slam. In that case, event organisers will have heard about you or seen you perform, and they may then invite you to feature. Or, if you've created a solid chunk of spoken word and audiences have responded well, you

CORPORATE CONFIDENCE

Here's an experience that isn't totally unique but it is rare. I asked a successful poet (who wanted to remain anonymous) if he did many gigs, considering his YouTube clips and TED talks have millions of views. He said, 'I'm on a fat drip feed from a large tech company doing corporate gigs.'

'When they first asked me, I didn't want to do it', the poet told me. 'So I asked them for $20000, thinking that would stop them. But it didn't. Suddenly I wanted to do it.

'But it got boring to the point where I just couldn't MC another Christmas party or feature at a "stockholder function", so I put my price up to $65000 a gig. Now I just do those five or six times a year and then I ... well, you know I like doing origami. But if I don't want to do something, I just ask for some crazy amount of money. If they say yes, then hey presto! Suddenly I'm motivated.'

can start approaching the organisers of slams and open mics to ask about doing a feature spot. If you want to cold call, though, you'll need to develop an online profile including photos, bio and video samples. The person on the other end of an email needs a reference point.

Pay for these spots depends on the size of the gig, the organisation hosting the event, your profile and your ability to negotiate. Have a look at the Australian Society of Authors' website (asauthors.org) for published rates for readings, teaching or sitting on panels. These are recommended rates for community organisations and for large cultural, governmental and educational organisations.

For corporate and major events, aim your price high and be prepared to come down. Ultimately, though, you do have to enlighten or entertain an audience for a good length of time before you think about quitting your day job.

MC or host

This a role that pays well and can be less demanding than long feature sets. You introduce other acts while sharing anecdotes, a couple of your own pieces and generally keeping the audience on their toes. You'll need to know how the particular slam or event runs, or get clear notes from the organisation that hires you. (See Chapter 5 for more information on running a slam.)

Going bigger

In the next chapter, we'll talk about setting up your own spoken word groups, gigs, slams and events. Just to give you a taste for it, here are some of the roles you could take on if you find that setting up performances is where you want to be.

Run workshops

Workshops are the butter on the bread of gigs. For all the spaces in between doing feature spots and hosting, there's teaching. Workshops can run from 1.5 hours to a full day. They can also be in the form of an 'artist in residence', where you're invited to teach and present over several days. The money for this usually pretty good but again it's good to consider the budget of the client.

I suggest 20 participants is a good maximum for a workshop, and 10–15 is ideal. Smaller groups will get more out of you. Remember that the organiser will take 10–30 per cent from participant fees to cover their costs. This applies to most gigs – you, the artist, are only one component of the event. The folks from the venue, doing the lights, selling tickets, doing publicity and filming the event all want to get paid. Make sure you factor all these people into the budget you set for a workshop.

I do run workshops for large groups, like 200 kids. It's good to do this with another facilitator if there is budget for it. The writers will need to work in teams, though. So you divide them up; there could be ten writers per group, or there could be four. Each person must contribute, for example, at least one line of poetry for large groups, four lines for smaller groups. They all add to their poems on butcher's paper. They underline words they will say together and circle words to echo. They must include at least one sound effect and one movement. One person acts as scribe. Then the whole group, or a minimum of two people from the group, perform the piece. They choose team names; you can give the

TRY THIS

SAMPLE WORKSHOP EXERCISES FOR PERFORMING WRITING

1 *Physical warm-up:* Start with a few laps around the room, some stretching, yawning, tongue twisters, humming, chanting, etc.

2 *Names:* Participants gather in a circle. They shout their first names, whisper their surnames and sing their middle names – first as a group, then as individuals.

3 *Aliens:* Participants close their eyes and imagine they are all from other planets: they each speak a completely unique language, move in a way that's unlike anything on Earth, and have a unique shape. When they open their eyes they must cross the room moving and speaking like their aliens.

4 *Gibberish:* Participants perform their poems in their alien gibberish. When someone yells 'English' they must switch to English.

See Part 3, pages 237–60, for more ideas for workshops.

teams fanfare announcements when they perform. The butcher's paper can be on the floor in front of the mic.

Workshops may be relatively expensive for participants when their numbers are limited – unless they're subsidised by grants or are part of in-house expenses for a company, festival or school.

Become a creative producer

With the current status of spoken word as a 'growing market', one of the key roles to consider is that of creative producer. In other words, start your own slam. You have to be somewhat entrepreneurial – it's a slow build to start at zero and get to the point where you can hire yourself out to deliver immersive creativity, but you'll get there. Build up a combination of funding, box office, sponsorship, donors, contract fees and more. In my role as a creative director, I'm now designing and directing full experiences – venue, artists, lighting, music – with a team. Early on, I got good at writing grant applications. Funding is the key. Look for it from grants and foundations.

If you want to go down this road, get an ABN – it's free – and it means you can invoice easily. You don't need to register for GST unless you earn over a certain amount. If you're going for large project funding, you'll need to either become an incorporated association by recruiting board members and sending in some paperwork to the Department of Fair Trading, or another organisation can vouch for you – that's called **auspicing**. The auspicing organisation will receive the money, sometimes charge a small percentage, then hand over the cash to you for your project. You always have to keep track of how the money was spent because in most cases you have to write a report when the project is finished. This is called an **acquittal**. This will also mean acknowledging funding bodies in whatever form they require and tracking how their brand was used.

There's more on starting a slam in Part 2 of this book. If you do go down this road, you'll find yourself learning sooo many things on the fly: from managing artists, web design, marketing and photography to the wild worlds of accounting software, office management and book-keeping. But the best thing about being a producer is that you can imagine all sorts of experiences that extend the idea of performing your writing and really engage communities.

The cool thing is that with more and more spoken word and poetry slam projects happening all over Australia, you won't be starting from zero. You'll be standing on the shoulders of a community. You can hope to surf the crowd and wind up on stage. In fact, if this book works, you *will* be on a stage and I *will* see you. So come say hello to the curly-haired dude sitting right up the front.

Where are you at?

At Word Travels, the literary arts organisation I founded, we have to decide who to hire for lots of different gigs. Among its many activities, Word Travels is an agent for spoken word artists.

We can't send out someone who's performed in one poetry slam to deliver a 2-hour mix of show and work-shop with 200 high school students or to a big corporate MC-ing gig. But we also get a bunch of small, one-off opportunities with tiny budgets that come to us and we don't want to turn those gigs down. So we have a pool

PRODUCE THIS!

Here are two examples of events I created for Story-Fest, the annual performing writers' festival that culminates in the Australian Poetry Slam's National Final.

Pin the tail on the station
A seven-step guide to trading places with your audience
Performance/Workshop/Field trip/Open mic
Timeframe: Varies
Audience: Maximum 20 people
Poets: 2–4

1   Audience meets poets at a train station.
2   Poets perform at the station.
3   One audience member is blindfolded and spun around three times in front of the rail map. Each time they stop, they point a finger at a station on the map. The audience then votes on which one of the locations they should go to.
4   Poets run a workshop on the train ride to the destination.
5   When they reach their destination, audience members gather artefacts and objects that represent the community they're visiting.
6   As they return to the original location by train, audience members write a spoken word piece based on the artefacts they chose.
7   Audience performs in open mic at the original train station.

Poet taster

Would you like a poem with that?

Performance

Timeframe: Varies

Performances: 2–3 minutes

Poets: Multiple

Audience: Variable; 1 to 8 – however many fit around a table, really

Poets will deliver their craft to audience members while they dine at a partnering restaurant or café.

Audience members choose a word when they pick up their drink or meal. A poet sits with each diner during their meal and shares a poem based on the chosen word.

No screens or devices allowed. Eye contact likely.

of artists that we contact, using the informal categories below.

- **Participant.** You've participated in a workshop, performed at an open mic, participated in one slam (not won) and/or recorded a video poem that under 100 people have watched.
- **Emerging.** You've performed in a few open mics, won a local slam and have a bit of online content. You can perform confidently with a memorised 20 minutes.

- **Developing**. At minimum, you've done a few feature spots and have a confident, memorised 30–60-minute repertoire including banter. You may have won a major slam. You have an obvious online presence. You have at least one video with over 1000 views, or you've published and sold copies of a book. You facilitate workshops.
- **Established**. This is your job. Your name on the bill will bring an audience. You can perform for over an hour for a variety of audiences. You've done several solo shows. You facilitate workshops.

BRANCHING OUT FROM SLAMS

'I've learned to write more openly and put more heart into my work as a result of this experience of participating in poetry slams ... I've now started drafting my first spoken word show that I'm performing at the Newcastle Fringe Festival. I also volunteer for a not-for-profit publisher partnering with The Wayside Chapel in Sydney. I will have the opportunity to mentor some of the Wayside poets who find poetry an important part of expressing their experiences. Having tapped into my vulnerable voice, I think I will be much better at helping others find their vulnerable voice too.'

Tiffany Harris, 2018 Australian Poetry Slam National Finalist

Who's hiring?

If you're not running your own event, then put your bio together with a couple of great images of you performing, and start sending emails and making calls. I like to call first, then email – so they're expecting the email. Use your imagination and pitch ideas to people or organisations you think have a budget, like:

- festivals
- schools – this is best done by an agent; there are a few who book artists into schools
- local libraries
- councils and government bodies
- youth centres
- private companies
- poetry slam organisers
- arts organisations
- advertising agencies.

Okay. You love performing your own writing or you don't. One thing's for certain: you love the vibe you get at a poetry slam and you just want to make it happen again and again – press repeat and grow some common unity in your community. Next up: you run this!

PART 2

SET UP
A SLAM

5

PLAN YOUR OWN EVENT

Here are some tips to help you set up your own gig, whether it's a slam, an open mic or a showcase event. (If you're setting up a slam or spoken word event for school students, see Chapter 9, pages 236–83 for a more specific guide.)

WHY SET UP AN EVENT?

'I was quite disengaged from school up until the end of Year 10. At that point, when I started running this open mic with a friend ... suddenly I had this thing to do, to wake up to and identify with. And while that existed outside of school for me, it flowed on into all other areas of my life. I suddenly became engaged and worked harder and saw the value of trying and doing things. Finding that thing, finding a reason to exist ... it flows on into everything else.'

Emily Crocker, poet and the
Rumble Youth Slam Champion

Location

First, you need a place to hold your spoken word event. This can be a formal venue, but it can also be a street corner, alcove, park or public space. (If it gets too big, you may have to inform your local council of your outdoor event – so let's start small.) Other options are cafés, bookshops, art centres, community halls, libraries, pubs … and the list goes on.

What you're looking for really is any space that will have you for free or pay you to put something on. Unless you already have a budget or expect to sell heaps of tickets, it's best to start with free or subsidised venues. Then move on to venues that will charge anywhere from a cut of the door (i.e. a percentage of ticket sales) to a few thousand dollars.

Another thing you can try is find a gig you like, in a venue you like, and set up a double bill with them.

Performers

In a slam or open mic, most of your performers will sign up on the night or online before the event. It's still good to think about a feature performer, someone who you know can Bring It. In your first event, it's likely that you will be the host, introducing all the acts, unless you find a friend. Hosts and featured performers expect to get paid – and rightly so. They see this as their job as well as their passion.

QUALITY COUNTS

'A slam or a poetry event is only as good as its poets. The more brave we can be, the more vulnerable, loving, powerful, connected and skilled, the better. Then, whether it's TV or movies or theatre or YouTube, the quality of the work will make the biggest difference. It doesn't matter about hits or views or likes, what matters is impact. If 20 people see your show but leave totally changed, that is so much more important for society than a video with a million views.'

Luka Lesson, spoken word poet, hip-hop artist, educator and 2011 Australian Poetry Slam Champion

If you're broke, you've got two choices: (1) charge money and offer a cut of the door, or (2) you host and feature at your own event. You can't do this every time but a one-off will work. A good plan is try to produce the first event under your own steam but take donations or charge a small fee for participation or entry, then use what you make to hire people for your next event.

Timing

If you're doing open mic or slam, you need to set a time limit for artists, and consider how many artists you're planning to invite on stage throughout the night. You don't want your event to be more than 3 hours long, with at least two 15-minute intervals.

Remember to schedule breaks. These are handy if you or your venue sells things. Nobody wants to order a coffee or buy a book in the middle of a vulnerable poetic outpouring.

Marketing and publicity

These are two different things. **Marketing** is you talking about your event. **Publicity** is getting other people to talk about it for you. Most of us find publicity more convincing than advertising.

The socials

The first thing you'll do is set up an online event using a social media platform of your choice. (At the time of writing this book, my preferred platform is a Facebook event.) Whichever platform you choose, there's no harm in hitting others – Instagram, Twitter, etc. – with posts about your event.

Does the venue have a website? Get on it. Find like-minded groups and send them links. Enter your event into 'What's On' listings for your local community.

Mail-outs

If you've got the emails of people you think want to know about your event (check your phone), set up an e-flyer/electronic direct mail (EDM) account on an online EDM platform – there are plenty of them around. Send an initial email to your email list to make sure they want to know about you. Once they've 'opted in', send an e-flyer.

Some platforms allow you to build a list of several thousand email addresses for free. You can also open several accounts.

There are heaps of templates for flyers available. Just throw in your image/s and an enticing event description and don't forget to include:

- the date
- the time
- the location
- the cost for audience/participants
- your contact details.

Bookings

Another good option if you're selling tickets or doing free but want folks to book is to use an event management technology platform (Eventbrite is a popular one). These platforms are pretty simple:

1   Put all that 'What's on' stuff into an event template.
2   Set up your box office.
3   Add your bank details.

4 Grab the link and share it wherever you're talking about your event online.

5 Watch the bookings roll in.

Website

Yes. You *can* build your own website. But when's the right time to go down that path?

I think right away, but it is one more thing you'll have to maintain. So keep it simple. There are free platforms and pay-per-month ones. Word Travels, Australian Poetry Slam and milesmerril.com are all built on Squarespace. My personal site took me about 3 hours to make. Shop around and find a template you like. Template sites are all drag, drop, click, write, save – no designer necessary. Just make sure you've got some amazing photos.

Your starter website could just be a two-pager that grows from 'About' and 'What's on' or 'Read-Watch-Listen' and 'Contact', to a combination of those four and then some. Merch anyone?

UPLOAD IT – FAST

When 12-year-old Solli Raphael won the Australian Poetry Slam in 2017, his mum designed and went live with a website for him within a couple of weeks.

Anyway, it's up to you. A website says that you're doing something professional. You have a home.

The paper stuff

Once you've done all the online sharing, decide if it's worth doing some paper flyers to hand out at your local festival or an event similar to yours (ask the organisers' permission and make sure the dates don't clash). You can place them in local cafés, libraries and bookshops (again, ask for permission). When you get super fancy, design a program with the schedule of the event, some photos, names of artists, sponsors, thank yous and list of people who worked on the gig.

Get them talking

Write a smart, brief, snappy, active press release to distribute to local papers, online news, radio stations even TV news. The best thing you can do in a press release is write the article you want them to publish – journalists are usually busy and may just do a cut-and-paste job into their publication. Boom! Free marketing. If they do contact you, they'll be looking for an interview with you and/or your key talent. Be ready to tell a story and control your message. Some journalists already know the story they want to tell. It might not be your story.

Either way, they will want to know more. They will definitely want high-resolution photos: 300 dpi is print quality. Check your image sizes. You want quality photos but try to keep each one under 4 MB unless you're asked for something bigger.

Equipment

Here are the seven things you need on stage for your own show. Check with the venue you're using and try to get as many of these as possible ticked off your list.

1: Amplifier (amp) or public address system (PA)

At any spoken word event, you want the audience to be able to hear the full dynamic range, from a whisper to a shout, so amplification is usually needed in a room of more than 30 people.

Formal venues usually come with a sound engineer and sound desk. The 'desk' is the thing with all the volume knobs and various holes that you plug your mic, instruments and effects pedals into. Have a chat with the sound person before the event and do a sound check.

Alternatively, you may just have a little amp or speaker that you bring, or that the venue owns. Plug your mic into the amp, turn it on, speak, adjust the volume and away you go.

Foldback speakers

An extra bit of equipment here is a set of foldback speakers, which face a performer on stage and allow them to gauge their own volume. They're particularly helpful in

MIC FRIGHT

Never stand in front of an amp with a mic. You'll get that loud, high-pitched squeal called feedback. Ouch!

larger venues and when musicians are performing. They allow performers to hear where their volume sits in the onstage mix.

2: Microphone

A cordless vocal mic – one that offers good-quality sound for vocals – is the best choice. (See pages 114–15 for more on mic options.)

3: Mic stand

A straight mic stand with a round base and clutch-grip height adjuster works best. The alternative option, a boom mic stand, is a little clumsier and can take up space (see pages 114–15). A straight mic stand with a clutch grip allows performers to slide the stand up and down for height adjustment instead of awkwardly twisting a cylinder.

4: Stool

A bar stool offers a little variety for performers to stand or sit.

5: Tall bar table or cocktail table

This is for performers' water and any additional items they bring on stage and want to access, like a device for music.

6: Jug of water and glasses

Prepare water jugs and glasses for performers, or offer to fill their own water bottles if they prefer. Don't offer plastic bottles of water. It's an environmental thing.

7: Audio cable

Provide a mini jack (or 3.5 mm) cable and input for an iPod/MP3 player. This is a standard auxiliary ('aux') cable that can fit into the headphone hole on a phone or whatever device performers use for music and can connect to your PA or amp.

You've got all your gear, done all the promo. It's time to pick up your mates. We're heading down to the venue.

6
ON THE DAY

The big day is here! Check out the sample guidelines in Appendix 2 for an idea of what your event might look like. Here's some more detail.

What you'll need

Ideally, you'll have at least three people to help with the event, including someone to help with the door if you're doing ticketing.

You'll also need some lists:

1   a pre-printed list of names for those who have booked online or in advance
2   a sign-up list for those who want to perform, plus 'hat slips' for determining the order of performers (see Appendix 4)
3   a sign-up list for those who want to join your mailing list.

Running order

You'll need a running order – a timed list of everything that happens on the night. It's handy for you, your featured performers and anyone else working on the event to have one of these. Include contact details of key people, but keep it confidential if you have artist contacts on there – only give it to those who need it. Distribute this via email prior to the event. It should have call times for crew and artists.

The standard call time for crew for a small event is 1–2 hours before doors open to allow for set-up. Call time for artists is usually 30–45 minutes before the start time, unless there is a scheduled sound check, in which case they can arrive during set-up (usually about 1–2 hours before doors open).

If you have people who are performing but don't need to know every detail on the running order, you can print them a short dot-point schedule or, if you're preparing a printed program for your audience, give those performers a copy of that.

For a sample running order, see Appendix 3.

Other things to bring

Remember to bring:

- your seven key items of equipment (see pages 152–54)
- two mates for slams:
  - a scorekeeper (see Appendix 5 for a scoring sheet)
  - a timekeeper, who will ding the warning bell at 1 minute 50 seconds

- your running order and sign-up sheets (see Appendixes 3 and 4)
- a stopwatch for the timekeeper
- a bell for the timekeeper to ding
- five mini-whiteboards with markers and erasers or cloths. Alternatively, a stack of paper and five markers divided between the five judges.
- three clipboards/folders for your running order and sign-up sheets
- pens for people to fill out the sign-up sheets
- an amount of cash in notes and coins that you use to give change; this is called the **float**
- a cash box, or bumbag with several pockets for cash
- a marker or a stamp to mark wrists
- a counter to keep count of attendees
- any merchandise you'd like to sell
- envelopes if you need to give cash to artists or competition winners (eventually you'll want to move to invoicing, online bank transfers and ABNs, but keep that in your back pocket for later)
- schedules for performers who don't need the running order
- audience programs, if you have them
- flyers for your next gig
- a camera and/or recording device to share video online – if you're planning to do this, draft a little paragraph that says, 'Here's how we're going to use this video – sign if you agree to this usage', and ask performers to sign
- a bag of chocolates or similar, for throwing into the

audience to select judges (give any extras away if you notice anyone's attention waning).

At the gig

Okay – you've set up the chairs, the merch table looks gorgeous, audio gear all plugged in, sound check checked. You (or a team member) welcome people at the door. Take their cash. Stamp their wrist. Wait 5–10 minutes after the start time to allow for stragglers. Cover up the merch table. MC takes the stage and opens with an Acknowledgment of Country. Then it's just … *listen*. That's the key thing, of course. The pay-off. You dive into the boring side of fun just so you can get to this moment. I've organised, attended or performed in very honestly thousands of spoken word events. It's listening to the poets that blows me away each time.

My partner and I were expecting our second daughter. The Australian Poetry Slam NSW final was in the first week of November, and the national final was the first week of December. My daughter was born on 20 November. Two weeks later, I found myself backstage at the Sydney Opera House, thinking: *What am I doing here? I should be home with my family.* It was the third poet to take the mic that got me. That poem snapped me back into the event and had me cheering inside. Every slam is different – different artists and forms of presenting; different passions; different levels of intricacy, insight and power. Because of this, I've never seen the same slam show twice.

Yes, you have tasks. If you're the organiser you might also be the MC/host. The MC of an open mic is pretty cruisy. Call people up. Be entertaining. Keep people to time. Listen. Chill. Say goodnight.

At a slam, if you're the MC, you are getting people to draw names from a hat, checking in with the timekeeper and scorekeeper. You're picking judges, getting scores from them. You're reading or reciting bios of features and throwing in a few poems of your own. The MC is the glue keeping the night going. It's their upbeat vibe; it's their ability to get the crowd excited and perform some of their own crowd-pleasing poems. They have to be humorous, knowledgeable and organised, with all the details of the event either memorised or in very clear notes.

If you're organising, you'll need to have a couple of people on the merchandise table and ticketing. This will require a float – an amount of money in small bills and coins to make change. You will ideally have a scorekeeper and timekeeper. You should have all of your sign-up sheets and documents printed and stuck on clipboards or in a folder, or have some electronic check-ins and sign-ups. The people who attend are going to be your mailing list. Also consider feedback forms or surveys. This will be helpful if this little gig o' yours starts to grow and you're thinking grants and funding. What's your impact?

You can do the event solo. Set up merch and sign-ups before the show; cover it during the show, uncover at intermission. Get audience or venue volunteers to

IT'S A COMMUNITY

'To have a group of poets and poetry lovers in a room on a weeknight celebrating creativity, storytelling and wordplay is my idea of perfect and I don't think you get that sense of community in many other areas of the arts.'

Lorin Elizabeth, spoken word poet and slam organiser

do scoring/timing. You can set up a video camera on a tripod and check it occasionally if you want to film your slam entrants. But it's much more fun to have friends help out.

After the gig

You're done! Don't forget to:

- collect feedback from people
- ask for volunteers to help out at the next event
- pay people
- clean up
- edit photos/videos/audio
- share the experience online
  ... and, last of all:
- promote the next one!

In 2017, I was hired by the Australian High Commission to travel to six cities in India, delivering workshops and performances in schools and at children's literature festivals. In Delhi, I asked my host from the high commission to bring her six-year-old son. I was performing in a park on a Sunday afternoon. She said, 'He can't go outside. He's allergic to the air.'

I went to my outdoor venue to perform. There were hundreds of kids, and half of them were wearing filter masks on their faces. When I started my trip, *The Guardian* reported the news that Delhi had been declared a 'gas chamber' due to air pollution from cars, coal and burning farmland after the harvest.

Seeing these kids and the poverty there – and in other places I visited, like Namibia, Zimbabwe and Jakarta – I thought: *What can you do? You're just a poet.* It still taunts me. *You're just a poet. So useless. What can you do.*

I don't know if this book will have an impact on you, or on people who appear as abstract statistics in poverty and climate change reports. But I have an idea to go where there is the most need and bring the mic to people whose stories need to be told.

An example: you might work with an education partner in Mumbai. Do performances in the slums; teach young people to perform their own poems, stories, lyrics and monologues; help them film each other, then share those bits of creative energy with the world. All this to create empathy for the experiences of people we may never otherwise encounter. Empower young people to the tell their stories.

That's why I've worked with Narcisa Nozica for two years to create this guide. Hopefully it becomes a resource for new performing writers, community organisers, teachers, youth workers and more. Hopefully this travels to places I can't. This is a transfer of knowledge. It's a pull-the-next-one-up.

PART 3

TEACH A REVOLUTION

7

WHY SPOKEN WORD?

Hannah Green, a graduate of Oak Park and River Forest High School in Chicago, joined her school's spoken word club in Year 10. In this club she found a supportive community and a sense of belonging. She was inspired and guided to write about her experiences poetically. She became a writer and a performer. Her poem 'Note to Dancers' illustrates exactly why we're here.

Note to Dancers

My sister was thirteen when she started
    counting calories
assumed if she wrenched her body smaller
maybe she'd take up more space on the stage
I sat in her dance recital and watched her
    firework into air
ladybug cheeks eclipsing the tundra of her
    shrinking face
as she bowed, hands laced together like the
    ribbon on her pointe shoes

I remember thinking how easy it is to break
   pencils in two.
So today I write a note to the dancers:
you are worth more than the angle of your hip
   in pirouette
we do not add teardrop waist to gaunt thigh
   and reach human
not getting the part because your chest is too
   big or hips too wide just means
you are evolutionarily woman
and women are not meant to be downsized

Hannah says:

I can't explain the type of community we formed
there. Everyone completely supported one another
as we shared some of our most difficult memories.
I met mentors and friends in this club. It's a
community I miss each and every day. This poem
specifically came out of my family's history of body
dysmorphia and eating disorders, issues I (along with
so many other women and men) continue to struggle
with. My oldest sister, one of my biggest role models,
was an avid dancer, and I saw how her community
ridiculed themselves in the mirror. Obviously, body
image is an issue both men and women struggle
with, but women are disproportionately affected by
it. In many aspects of our lives, women are taught to
make themselves smaller, and this was a cry against
those forces.

MY FIRST TIME

My first experience of spoken word poetry was a revelation. It was a local heat of the Australian Poetry Slam, in a small pub. The mood was electric, the poets mind blowing. The next day I just had to try my hand at a little writing myself. (I'd later realise that this is a common side effect of seeing spoken word live.) It dawned on me that this would be an awesome way to teach poetry.

I started the first lesson of the next year's Year 9 poetry unit by performing this piece. I didn't introduce the topic. I just got up and dove right in.

> I am an acrobat
>> Before the show, I stretch the hamstrings
>>> and the calves of my soul,
>> I soften and fold,
>> ready to let go
>
>> The tight-wire stands before me.
>> At its end I see freedom but first,
> first I walk ...

Afterwards I asked the class what they thought I was doing. Instinctively they knew it was a poem, and – shockingly – *they wanted more*. That day, I ignited a small flame: not just within the students, whose perception of poetry was utterly transformed, but within me, to find a new way to teach it.

NARCISA

This part of *Slam Your Poetry* is for teachers, poets, community workers and leaders who are looking for a way to make change. To change the way people in their communities and classrooms see themselves. To change the way they see, understand and feel about poetry. To change the way people in their communities interact. Spoken word gives us tools to educate, connect and empower.

Changing minds, lives and communities

Spoken word poetry puts individual voices and experiences at the centre. When people, especially young people, realise they don't have to be wordsmiths to be valued for their artistry, magic happens. When they read poetry in which they can hear and see themselves, they learn to love it.

For young people, whose literacy skills are still developing, getting the opportunity and the tools to tell their own stories means they become more invested in their own literacy. Academics, and their research, agree. Susan Weinstein, an American university teacher, researcher and author, has been working with young poets and studying the astonishing effect spoken word has on them. She believes that the most effective way into poetry is to teach young people 'as writers': 'Kids engage much more with something when they're positioned as people who are doing that thing.'

This is why, in spoken word workshops, there are no students. There are only writers.

IGNITING THE SPARK

Troy Wong, a Sydney-based English teacher and poet, says: 'A lot of the kids in my school don't see themselves as readers, as skilled with language, and many of them don't read for fun. When you're educating them in the mastery of language ... it has to be relevant, there has to be some kind of *spark* before you can get any traction.'

He recalls one lesson with a Year 7 class in which he first showed a spoken word poem video to students. 'When they saw it, they lit up', he says. 'Some of the boys said, "That poem said what I already feel. I want to be able to do that."'

Giving people a voice

Spoken word poetry programs offer something unique and special: an opportunity for people to explore and express themselves and their world. This opportunity is perfect for young people, a group in great need of confidence, purpose, self-esteem, belonging and healing. It acts almost as a supportive parent, welcoming all with open arms and mending the spirit with the simple act of giving them their voice.

Two dedicated spoken word teachers, Peter Kahn and Adam Levin, work with students in Chicago to write poetry. One of those students, Jesus Govea IV, wrote the poem 'Bleeding into Grass', which shows us how the

spoken word program helped him use symbols, meta-
phors and imagery to wring out painful experiences and
transform them into something beautiful.

Bleeding into Grass

At my grandma's house,
I stepped on glass before.

The blood on my foot
a splinter for smooth sand soles.

I remember when my dad
tried to remove it.

For some reason,
all my uncles and aunts were there.

Eyes shifting around
a little boy with a heel that screamed maroon.

Holding me down
my father twisted tweezer with snapping
    incisors into my foot.

I'm going to have a heart attack
split its way up my throat.

Rusted hands prying
lip, teeth, and tongue apart.

Why spoken word?

I've never been more afraid of shattered glass
since.

But
that's all that I pick up lately.

Pieces of moonlight at my feet.
Each cutting reflections of the things I must do.

The grades I must file down, the list of colleges
    I have to sweep up,
and the crystalled eyes of a girl who I have to
    forget.

Every rigid slice nibbling into my palm,
the stinging mirages pooling at its center.

I never knew something so fragile can break
    skin.
Or responsibilities so sturdy can fall apart at
    your fingertips.

How can I chew glass when I have trouble
    swallowing my own spit.

Although I heal
cause the ink of my pen licks my wounds.

Each stroke of stanza
a stitch of blotched kisses.

Sterile syllables disinfecting
the scum in my palm lines.

Leaving my body radiant.
Moonpied and plump.
Knowing that these shards aren't the only thing
I can bleed into.

When I got the chance to talk to some of the kids in the Spoken Word Club run by Peter and Adam, I found out that their spoken word program literally saves lives. It lifted one student out of apathy and depression towards straight As. Why? Because it made him realise that his life and his voice mattered. This is not an isolated example.

A LIFELINE

'I got a handwritten note from a graduating student one time. She said, "I think poetry kept me in the world last year."'

Simon Kindt,
English teacher and poet

WRITING BONDS

The ability of spoken word groups to bond at lightning speed is remarkable. When establishing my own spoken word family at Blakehurst High School, it took less than 2 hours. Yes, 2 HOURS! Within that time, students started sharing intimate details about themselves, their mental health, their struggle with parental expectations, their self-esteem, their sexual orientation, their traumatic pasts, their political beliefs and more.

As we met outside the library for the second session, I watched them greet each other. One student bounced up to the group and shouted, 'Hey, family!' It was already happening. They were listening to each other, supporting each other and writing deeply personal stuff. The writing community establishes roots quickly, especially if those roots are watered by the group's facilitator.

NARCISA

Other students have told me how writing to perform helped them overcome stage fright and gave them confidence that they carried into other parts of their lives. They often described how spoken word becomes an outlet to vent frustrations, cope with difficulties and move on. Brianna, a Sydney high school student, explains:

> A lot of my poems reflect time periods in my life. I look back on them and, even when they weren't the best, it's good to reflect on them and think about how I moved past that, so it's definitely emotionally fulfilling. It's like putting it in a box, to the left. I've articulated how I felt about this, so now I can move on.

A spoken word club is also a place to make and solidify friendships and discover a sense of belonging.

A new sense of self

Last, and maybe most important of all, is the effect on identity. Research has shown that spoken word programs help young people develop a positive and productive identity as writers and performers who are part of an artistic community. Their new *literary* identity boosts their self-confidence. When they take risks, like experimenting with language or performing in front of an audience, they receive positive feedback and support. This helps them develop the emotional resilience that allows them to tackle life, including its setbacks, head on.

TAPPING INTO FEELINGS

'I've heard Mahogany L Browne say it's not therapy, but it's therapeutic. Being human, we all feel emotions that often go by so fast we've no time to process them, so a class on spoken word is often a class on personal development. I hope we're teaching critical thinking; for students to be able to see and recognise the value that words have.'

Jon Sands, teaching artist

Harnessing this power in a classroom, in a school program or out in the community could be the key to unlocking young people's sense of power in their lives.

What teachers can do

In my quest to find out how other teachers have harnessed the power of spoken word, I came across Simon Kindt, a poet and English teacher from Queensland. Simon had discovered the power of live performance to inspire his students. He invited American poet Bill Moran, known for his imagery-charged, rhythmic poetry, to perform at his school and has used this partnership to build a cutting-edge extracurricular program.

To understand the power of programs like this, we only need to read the poems that students produce. Tahlia McConochie was one student who benefited from the program:

> It was one teacher's encouragement that pushed me to really give poetry a go, and once I did, it was another's support from very early on that motivated me to keep writing. While I was in school, poetry became a very rewarding passion, an emotional outlet, and afforded me a comfortable, solid place in the school community. Today, poetry is a close friend of mine.

Tahlia's poem, below, 'developed from an idea of an estranged Jesus Christ', she says, and 'considers religion in a world that perhaps no longer needs it'.

He, with no more pressing matter to pursue

He lifts his head like a handbrake
in the centre of one freezing suburban
   McDonald's;
where the ground is as sticky and stained as it
   is dull.

With leaves in his hair and red in all the cracks
   of his level swipe of teeth,
there's Sun all caught up on his temple,

hanging there like a dried towel on the back of
    a fold-out chair,
and red swimming its pretty body down his
    edges.

He offers to pay for my food
as I fold and deposit the
fries
that I already bought
into my mouth.

There's salt on my fingers when he takes them
    to tell me something
big
There are splinters in his
and dirt settled into the borders.

"You look better than you did the other day,"
he says,
brightly, squeezing my hands so my fingers
    feel just too full.
And I look away,
at the bored looking cashier
who wears her hair tumbling down her
    shoulder;
and at the cream coloured lines
stretching their new fingers through the
    leather
between and around my thighs.

"The good was there before,"
he assures.
He shakes his hair and crumbs of earthly
    matter
descend
onto the white of the table.
"It was being interrupted,"
he chews,
"partially covered, maybe."

He offers to pay for me again
with a hand outstretched like a crane jib and
beckoning my agreement
but,
in an aside made only to myself
and telepathically to the bored looking cashier,
who by this point has no more pressing matter
    to pursue than to watch this muted scene
    unfold,
I note that he has no money on him.

Dirty and almost completely naked
in the centre of one freezing suburban
    McDonald's;
where the ground is as sticky and stained as it
    is dull.

POETRY ON THE MOVE

'The research shows that the programs that have been in place for a while overseas, in the UK and the US, have a really positive flow-on effect in terms of life-long literacy and learning ...Young people are now buying poetry books in much greater numbers than any other part of the population ... 18–25-year-olds are supporting much great growth in the poetry publication industry.'

Sarah Temporal, poet and teacher

Spoken word in schools

If you're a teacher, you may be asking whether spoken word poetry has any academic benefit. How does it fit into what is most likely a dense curriculum, whether that be English, Drama, Personal development and health, or even History?

The research says the benefits are real. Spoken word programs improve school attendance and retention; they help kids want to stay at school. They also improve overall academic performance. When a student becomes personally invested in a school program, they start to pay a lot more attention to other parts of their schooling. This

CREATIVE SPACE

'There's a time and a place for dictating and giving the notes, there's a time and place for preparing students for an exam, but any space we can carve out that allows them to experiment and be creative, the happier the kids are. And if they're happy at school, we've got them. Then you can do whatever you like!'

Penny Horsley, English teacher

is true whether the program is associated with school or not!

Exposure to the words and styles of performing writers is always key to a spoken word writing community. These poetry models inspire ideas, and demonstrate artistic craft and technique. They broaden vocabulary and promote critical thinking.

Something else happens too. As students listen to other poets' words, they recognise that this is *now* – it's real and it's raw – and this makes them really listen. There's a light bulb moment. Students begin to appreciate wordplay and language, and that appreciation turns them onto paying much closer attention to what they are reading and writing. A deeper understanding of artistic craft follows.

In a school spoken word program, students are encouraged to write and rewrite. And rewrite. And rewrite! This is then shared with the group, and here is where spoken word makes the biggest difference to literacy: when a student knows a work will be shared or performed, their motivation to draft and edit increases. As high school student Brianna expresses it, 'The competition gives incentive to work really, really hard ... It makes people put themselves in the poetry and work on it to the last letter.'

Spoken word is perfect for students of all levels of writing and reading ability. Spelling, punctuation and grammar can take a back seat, while word choice, sequencing, poetic devices, narrative devices and form take the spotlight. Despite – or maybe even because of – the lack of focus on the nitty-gritty detail, it helps them make language theirs.

Syllabus links

But what about the syllabus? Spoken word nestles easily into the **English** syllabus in its emphasis on the appreciation of the richness and power of language and literature. The syllabus asks teachers to 'create confident communicators, imaginative thinkers and informed citizens'. When a student participates in spoken word, they learn so much about how English works in its spoken, written and non-linguistic forms. They learn how to make meaning in a new and exciting way. They develop fluency in reading and listening to one of the most diverse

CHECK YOUR ASSUMPTIONS

I'm working in a drop-in youth centre. For an hour, I let the kids show me what they like doing, and I do it with them – dance, play music, play basketball, rap, practise the acrobatics they learned from the circus trainers last year.

Then, in the second hour, I kick off the workshop. 'Okay, thanks guys, that was pretty awesome. Now I'd like to show you what I like doing and we can all do it together. It's really simple. I'm going to put on an instrumental track and all I want you to do is write about whatever you did last night using your senses. What did you see, hear, taste, touch, smell? The track only goes for five min–'

'Uh sir', one kid interrupts, raising his hand. 'I gotta go use the toilet.'

Another hand shoots into the air. 'Sir, yeah, uh me too.'

Two more hands shoot up.

'Okay', I say. 'We'll take a little break and come right back, eh?'

The whole group gets up to 'use the toilet'. Of the 15 kids, only seven come back. The others walk out of the room, turn right to the basketball court and start shooting.

I turn to the youth worker, Darryl, who hired me. 'What should I do?' I ask him, out of earshot of the boys.

'Well, you've just embarrassed those boys. None of them can write.'

I couldn't believe it. 'But it's a writing workshop. Why did you hire me? What am I supposed ...'

'I don't know. Figure it out, I guess?'

'Okay, but these guys here?' I point to the seven seated boys, aged between 10 and 18.

'They're all good. They can write,' Darryl says.

I have an idea. A game. Darryl encourages the boys to come back in.

They're all seated in a semi-circle in blue plastic chairs.

'Okay guys.' I'm looking at the kids who had walked out. 'You are superstars. Superstar basketball or footy players – whatever you want to be. You are the best. You are so incredible that you're being interviewed on the TV news. By these guys over here.'

I point toward the other seven kids. 'These guys are journalists. They're gonna interview you and write down your answers. They're going to write your story down. The theme is "My Big Night". It can be last night, it can be last weekend, it can be your best or worst night ever. You can make it up. Use your imagination. There can be dragons – whatever you want. These guys are gonna capture your story. Cool?'

Each of the boys who 5 minutes earlier had raced out of the room pairs up with a 'journalist'. One of them pairs with Darryl. I walk around prodding ('Journos, make sure you put in punctuation: full stops, commas, quotations and question marks.'), offering encouragement, answering questions and mostly listening. What I hear are great stories told using all the literary tools – metaphors, suspense, images of action, rhythm, characters, dialogue. Their ability to tell a story leaps over the limitations of literacy.

I ask the 'journalists' to read what they've written back to the 'superstars'.

I see intense listening and pride. And I hear conversations:

'Nah, I think I kind of stopped there and did this little spinning movement with my hand. Can you put the spinning in?'

'Could you go back? You're reading it too fast. I think I had a bit of a pause after that last bit. Yeah. I think sir said that's a comma?'

These guys are getting invested in their own experiences and trying to make sure their story is told properly. I see that through the immediacy and accessibility of the spoken word, these kids gain an avenue into literacy where their self-esteem gets boosted, and the desire to tell a better story becomes a serious goal.

MILES

forms of expression. They innovate in their own writing. English teachers could easily meet some key outcomes by developing a spoken word unit of work, choosing a broad theme to work within, like 'Passionate Poetry' or 'Protest Poetry', or something with a more specific lens like gender, culture or sustainability.

Spoken word can work well in **History**, as students respond to current or historical events, or examine the responses of others. You could have students write poems in response to the historical events and situations they are learning about. The performance aspect allows it to be easily embedded in an arts curriculum, including **Drama** and **Music**.

It also has great potential in **Personal development and health** as a way of exploring a range of physical and mental health issues and relationships, as well as offering students another personal coping strategy for everyday life. For example, you could embed spoken word poetry into lessons on human relationships.

Through careful text and topic selection, spoken word is a meaningful way to meet the **cross-curriculum priorities** and **general capabilities** outlined in every syllabus, from intercultural understanding to sustainability! Its use in schools is only limited by the teacher's imagination.

Spoken word in the community

There's a good reason why spoken word has been used successfully in community programs, especially outreach.

It has the potential to transform how a person sees themselves, how they perceive and connect to other people in their lives and how they participate in their communities. Spoken word is for anyone who feels voiceless, who lacks confidence or a sense of purpose, or who needs an outlet for emotions and experiences. It's also for those who want to be part of something, to feel like they belong to a community, to have a little fun!

Let's not forget that it's also about the poetry – for the aspiring wordsmiths who need a little help to free the imaginative spirit.

Spoken word programs can be run in so many different parts of a community, such as community arts centres, outreach centres, hospitals, aged care homes and facilities, church groups, support groups for people with illnesses and addictions, detention centres for asylum seekers, prisons and so many more.

All of the tips and tricks you're about to read in Chapter 8 will be useful in a school program or a community program. Remember to keep an open mind, don't assume anything and be flexible. Respond to what and who you have in your group (just as Miles did in the story above). But first you'll need a little planning.

8

ENGAGE YOUR WRITERS

Let's get started. The five ideas in this chapter will help you set up the structures, routines and rituals needed to engage a group of novice performing writers in spoken word.

Create a spoken word community

A spoken word community, whether it's an arts or community group or an extracurricular group at a school (like a lunchtime club), gives new poets the opportunity to hone their writing and performing skills and grow closer together. The supportiveness of that community, and their own growth as writers, will keep them coming back.

Tips for establishing a writing group

- Open the group to as diverse a range of people or students as possible.
- Give the group a fun name, or even better, leave the naming up to the group.

- Set up a special, intimate space for writing, sharing and performing. There should be a space (ideally a circle) where you guide discussion, look at model poems and brainstorm. Then, you can have the writers 'break out' and find their own private space for writing. Have a makeshift stage for performing.
- Involve the group in the program – ask them to bring links to favourite spoken word videos or copies of favourite poems.
- Invite working poets to perform for them, deliver workshops and work with individuals on their poems.
- You can promote the group by holding a special event (at a school, writers' festival, local council event or community event).

Tips for writing groups in schools

In addition to the tips above, if you're working in a school you can also try these:

- Invite a poet to perform.
- Show spoken word videos during school assemblies and year meetings, and in classes.
- Ask existing members of the writing group to perform for classes, year levels or the whole school.
- Run an all day spoken word event, including workshops and a slam.
- Take the group to a live poetry slam.
- Partner with other schools, work on a program

together and/or conclude the program with a local school slam or showcase. Some states have programs like this already running, like Australian Poetry Slam Youth (NSW), OutLoud (Vic), SlammED (Qld) and others. (See 'Further reading' for links.)

- Celebrate student achievement through a performance evening, a showcase, a published chapbook or videos (see 'Put on a show' in Chapter 9 for ideas.)
- Embed spoken word in the curriculum by adjusting or creating a new unit of work (see 'Syllabus links' in Chapter 7).
- Work in explicit teaching of poetic and narrative devices through careful selection of model poems.
- Develop an anthology of model poems that students can read during class time, club meetings and workshops, and at home. (There's more about model poems in the chapters to come.)

NOT A NORMAL CLASS

'It's important for there to be a distinction between "This is an English class" and "This is a writing workshop" ... You need to design it with a different atmosphere in mind ... Try to denaturalise that teacher role as much as possible.'

Simon Kindt, English teacher and poet

A note on assessment

If you're incorporating spoken word into your curriculum, consider assessing the writing *process*, rather than the product. One example is a composition folio that includes a poem at various stages of development, with a reflection statement that explores the student's development as a writer and refers to their own work. Or students could include several works written at various stages that showcase their experimentation with language, their growth and their deepened understanding.

You might be tempted to ask students to submit a writing journal if they have one (see page 195) as part of their assessment, but if you want this journal to be their 'safe space' for personal thoughts and experimentation with words, I recommend against it. They can use their journal to help them write a more formal reflection statement on their progress.

The first session (or two)

By far, the best introduction to poetry a new poet can have is to witness a live performance that is pitched at their level – something funny but powerful, something that challenges their preconceived notions about poetry being stuffy, formal or simply alien to them.

Bring in a poet if you can. At Blakehurst High School, for example, we like to invite a poet (thanks, Miles!) to kick off our spoken word program. We pour all the kids into the school library and they sit down, expecting to be bored and to try to sneak in as much whispering and phone time as possible while the teachers' backs are turned. Miles starts with his special brand of humming and throat clearing into the microphone. You can see the students looking at each other, like, 'What's this?!' Then he weaves stories of other kids writing poems in with his own works, exploring his personal experiences of racism and tailoring his presentation according to what the group needs. He gets the kids participating, and before you know it they're walking out with a totally new understanding of what poetry is and telling us they're looking forward to more!

If you can't bring in a poet, take the group to a show. Or perform something yourself. Do whatever you have to do to give the poetry life.

Videos

The next best introduction to poetry is a carefully curated selection of poems on YouTube. Here are some of my favourites, for starters, below (see links, Appendix 1). There are more suggestions on choosing model poems in the section 'Choose poems that stoke the fire', later on.

Daniel Beaty, 'Knock Knock'

This one's a cracker. Daniel Beaty gives a riveting performance about losing his father and inspires the audience members to make their own destiny. I like this one because of the sheer strength of his delivery and the passion of his words.

Marshall Davis Jones, 'Spelling Father'

This one was so popular across social media that the poet was given the opportunity to perform it at TEDx. Jones tells the story of a dream in which he misspells the word 'father' at a spelling bee, spelling it 'm-o-t-h-e-r' instead. I use it with kids aged 14 and over because of the way Jones flips our expectations of words to honour his mother.

Melanie Mununggurr-Williams, 'I Run'

This one is a great choice for high school students and adults, and especially good for a culturally diverse group because the poet was the first ever Aboriginal Australian poet to win the Australian Poetry Slam. At first Mununggurr-Williams uses everyday language to talk about everyday experiences, making the poem easily accessible, but as it continues she seamlessly weaves in powerful imagery to explore personal experiences and wider social issues. It does contain some swear words.

Arielle Cottingham, 'Tramlines'

For an older or more academically minded group, I really love 'Tramlines'. The poet explores her struggle to be accepted by her religious family as gay through the metaphor of straightening her curly hair.

Neil Hilborn, 'OCD'

Neil Hilborn has been a favourite among my students. I like this poem not only because it talks about a very personal battle with obsessive-compulsive disorder, but because it is a love story. The performance is powerful, making use of sound, movement, repetition and tone to make the audience really understand the experience of OCD.

Mike Taylor, 'Thinking About You'

This one is great for teens who can't see the point of poetry and have decided that they definitely can't (and don't want to) write it. Mike Taylor will change their minds.

Candy Royalle, 'Love'

This one is heartbreaking and inspiring all at once. I usually like to use it with older groups when I want to show them an example of why people write and share poetry. The late Candy Royalle defies her impending battle against ovarian cancer by shaving off her hair and performing this poem about what really matters in life.

Candy Bowers, 'Australia, I love you. But ...'

I love this poem for a diverse group, particularly for girls, as it talks about body image and the lack of representation of women of colour in Australia's media. The language is everyday and highly accessible. It does contain some swearing, but it is used for effect.

Define it

Another way to introduce poetry to a new writing group is to tackle the definition head-on.

TEACH THIS

WHAT IS POETRY?

Here are some ideas for introducing poetry in early group sessions.

- Discuss what group members think a poem is. Give them post-it notes and ask them to write the end of the sentence, 'A poem is ...' Stick them to a whiteboard or wall, check them for appropriateness and have one group member read them all out. Use their responses as a discussion starter. (This might be a good end-of-program activity too, to see how far your poets have come in their thinking and attitude towards poetry.)
- View the 'Understanding poetry' clip from the film *Dead Poets Society* (see link, Appendix 1) and discuss what poetry is, what it's for, how it can be used, and how it should be read and appreciated.
- Read Billy Collins's poem 'Introduction to Poetry' (see link, Appendix 1) and discuss. Use it as a preamble to explain to your new writers that the poems you will read together will not be 'beaten' for meaning, but used as inspiration. You will be asking them to connect to the poems and tell you what *they* think.

The writing journal

You can encourage the members of the group to have a special writing journal. In this journal they can brainstorm, illustrate, paste, copy favourite phrases or poems, research, free-write, draft and edit.

At the back of the journal I strongly recommend adding a **Writer's Toolbox**. During sessions, whenever an interesting word, useful phrase or literary element or device comes up, ask your group to add it to the Toolbox for future reference. Words like *stanza*, *ellipsis* and *metaphor* can be added in over time, but they could also add in tips and strategies for performance they have learned from the poets they have watched. Refer back to it when discussing other poems or when you have prompted a new piece of writing.

To reinforce this, you can put up a large poster at the back of the room, or create a shared document online in which you keep a group version of the Toolbox.

WRITE IT DOWN

Encourage your writers to always have pen and paper on hand (or a smartphone notes app) so they can jot down ideas and additions to their Toolbox wherever they are.

Sculpt your workshops

The bread and butter for any teacher or teaching artist in a writing group is the workshop. Each session with your group should cover one or more parts of the workshop scaffold below, which can be structured or sequenced in many different ways. The scaffold is based primarily on the model I observed in use by Young Chicago Authors, a spoken word non-profit organisation.

Initially, you will want to infuse your workshops with fun. Try playing a game at the beginning of sessions to build confidence and interest in writing. (For game ideas, see pages 198–201.)

Workshop scaffold

1 **Break the ice**
   Social icebreakers, games and free-writing exercises.
2 **Model the writing**
   Show a performance of a model poem or read a poem out loud.
   Dig into the model
   Facilitate a group-led discussion of the model poem, digging into its content and/or a focal feature.
   and/or
   Talk it out
   Alternatively, or in addition to modelling, start with a group discussion of a topic that is relevant to writers' experiences or feelings, or accesses their knowledge, attitudes or beliefs.

3 **Scaffold the writing**

Give a series of quick, accessible writing prompts, such as brainstorms, questions or lists. Make these both broad and specific, to ensure every poet will have something to connect with. This will give them a bank of ideas and words to use for immediate writing.

4 **Draft poetry**

Prompt poets to draft a poem, inspired by an element from the writing prompts and the model poem. Provide further scaffolding where needed. Poets can compose individually or collaboratively, in pairs or groups.

5 **Share**

Encourage all poets to share their pieces with the group, finished or not.

6 **Feed it back**

Poets and facilitator provide feedback – praise, suggestions and questions to consider.

7 **Revise**

Review and edit the draft poems.

8 **Rehearse**

Practise performing the poems.

9 **Perform**

Provide an opportunity for poets to perform their work before a live audience.

WORDPLAY

'Lots of wordplay exercises work well ... Students really enjoy playing around with words and seeing what other meanings come out, and how easily you can make something sound interesting or bring up ideas that you didn't know were there, by doing things like breaking words apart and putting them back together or playing around with rhymes.'

Sarah Temporal, poet and teacher

Games for getting started

Let's look at some ideas for games that work well as ice-breakers or no-pressure workshops, perfect for the early weeks of a spoken word program. (There are more ideas for icebreakers on pages 218 and 219.)

It's Magnetic

In small groups, give poets a cluster of words from a magnetic poetry kit. The challenge is to create a poem using all, a specific number, or a percentage of the words (for the added numeracy challenge). Groups can then take a tour around the room to see the other poems, or you can put them all up on a whiteboard.

Post-it Poets

Give each poet one post-it note, on which they write a response to a refrain you have provided. For example, you write a sentence-starter like 'I remember …' or 'At first …' or 'Everything changed when …' on a board. All poets write their own ending to the sentence.

Assign one poet to represent the beginning and end of the poem. This poet simply repeats the sentence-starter you have provided at the start and end. Each group member stands to say their line ('I remember when I first arrived', and so on), one after another.

Next, ask the group to rearrange all the poets and their lines to make the poem flow, then repeat the performance.

To create a more consistent tone or cohesive poem, start the session by discussing a specific topic or experience to generate a particular mood in the group, or to get them reflecting on similar subjects.

Blackout Poetry

Photocopy a variety of pages from a book and give poets pencils and black markers. They create a poem out of the words on the page by blacking out the words they don't want to use. Suggest they start by using a pencil to put a box around the words they like and challenge them to work on it until they've created a coherent poem. They can even use a variety of colours and create a picture on the page. Blackout Poetry is a popular form and many examples can be found online to show your writers.

- **As an editing tool:** Poets can also use this technique on their own poetry to craft more sharp and powerful pieces. They bring in a poem they've written and black it out to its core, or down to the most beautiful or powerful words. They can even use this as a new starting point for their poem, beginning with the strongest imagery or phrases.

Beat Poetry

Borrow some drumsticks or find a free-to-use hip-hop beat from a website like SoundCloud. Poets write a poem to perform to the beat or over the beat. Alternatively, you can give them a poem and ask them to perform it to the beat. Best performance wins a prize!

Paddle-pop Poetry

Another group game. Using dictionaries (hard copy or digital) – or, if you're working in a school, you can use a vocabulary list from a book or topic – groups of poets select around 15 words and copy them onto paddle-pop sticks. You can restrict it to just nouns, adjectives, adverbs or verbs, or include a mix. Each group swaps its paddle-pops with another group's (but don't tell them in advance that this will happen) and writes a poem using at least ten of the sticks. They are allowed to add prepositions, pronouns and other small words to make the poem flow. Each group performs their piece to raucous applause.

- **As an editing tool:** Poets can examine the word choice in their poem or another group's poem, and make changes to make a more powerful piece.

Partner with poets

Partnerships with poets, particularly through week- or month-long residencies that include ongoing work with the same established poet and your group of new poets, are the best gift you can offer your group. If you're a teacher or community worker, you might have an air of authority that can distance you from your group. A spoken word program can have much more impact when a bona fide poet works with the group. Young poets are more open to listening to and learning from teaching artists and are more likely to follow in the footsteps of these role models.

You can find poets through a simple search online for spoken word poets or workshops in your city. You can also find a poet you like through YouTube, then look for their website or social media account. Then just contact the poet directly, who may direct you to their agent. Organisations like Word Travels can also arrange opportunities like this, while poets from other countries might be willing to Skype with you.

An alternative, one that teaching artist Sarah Temporal has used successfully, is to tap into an existing network of poets in your local community. Look for an open mic night or a slam – they're often held in pubs, cafés or libraries – and make contact with the poets there. They may be able to talk with your writers about why they love poetry and the techniques they use, and inspire the group through a live performance.

The beauty of poet partnerships is that the poet can offer ideas from a writer's perspective that can help budding poets flourish, poetically and personally. Bill Moran, working with Simon Kindt at a school in Queensland, inspired a group of students to find the wordsmith within. As one of those students, Megan McMahon, explains:

> I wrote '5 Cent Coin' when I was 15. It was the second spoken word poem I had ever written and performed. When I wrote it, it was meant to be a poem about valuing people for who they are as opposed valuing them for who they are compared to ... I remember [after performing it], some of the older students coming up and complimenting me, and telling me what the poem meant to them. I remember thinking how awesome it was that my poem had meant something different to everyone there. Some thought it was literally about the value of money, while others saw it as a poem about self-worth ...
>
> Poetry and spoken word performance plays such a big role in my life today, and without this poem and the opportunities that learning performance poetry in high school gave me, I don't know where I would have ended up.

5 Cent Coin

Boy picks up 5 cent coin.
Thinks he's rich.
Slips it into his lint filled, stolen lolly wrapper
    stuffed pockets and saves it for a day when
    he can buy the world.

Boy comes home from school, rivers on his
    cheeks and rivers in his knees.
Boy is not useless.
Boy is not worthless.
Boy turns his pockets inside out to prove them
    all wrong.
5 cent coin, glistens silver, glows starlight in his
    grazed scarlet palm.
Boy finds hope.
Holds it close.
Boy believes he can be rich.

Boy drops 5 cent coin.
Boy drops his hands, boy drops his knees,
    boy drops his eyes, boy embraces his pirate
    side, not caring, not even feeling the spears
    of judgment thrown at his bowed back by
    passing eyes.
Boy finds 5 cent coin.
Holds it close.
Boy believes he can be rich.

SLAM YOUR POETRY

Boy finds dollar coin.
And it's bigger, and it's better, and it's shinier,
    and it's gold like the treasure of a king!

Boy finds dollar coin.
Thinks he's rich.

5 cent coin gets pushed into the crinkled
    corner.
The teeth slam shut, smothering value, hiding
    its worth.

Boy finds 50 cents.
Boy finds 2 dollars.
Boy finds three 20's.
Boy finds a blue note with a big old 10 on it!

Boy drops 5 cent coin.
Boy drops his eyes, then picks them up again.

5 cent coin is old.
5 cent coin is tarnished.
5 cent coin is worthless.
5 cent coin won't get him anything, won't get
    him anywhere.
5 cent coin won't make him rich.
Doesn't even make him feel rich.
Not anymore.

5 cent coin is left behind.

5 cent coin lies alone, unnoticed on the
    concrete side walk, dying silver turning grey,
    bullied to blend in.
5 cent coin dreams of being picked up and
    thrown into wishing well, just so it may
    hope to be worth something, to be worth
    anything, to anyone.
One last time.

Girl picks up 5 cent coin.
Polishes grey on cotton and reveals silver.
Girl holds 5 cent coin up to the sky, blocking
    out the gold.
The blues and greens and yellows and reds
    fade away and lose their meaning.

Girl holds up 5 cent coin, and sees herself.
And she smiles.

Tips on developing a poet partnership

- Try to match the poet's energy and style with your group's dynamic. You want the poet to be inspiring but not to overshadow the new poets.
- Balance the poet's time between performing for the group to inspire and model, delivering workshops to small groups, working with individual participants,

and hosting an open mic, showcase or slam. The focus should still remain on your writers.

- Be specific about what you need from the poet. Do you want the poet to:
  - embed the program with a specific unit of work or topic?
  - cover certain aspects of writing and/or performing (for example, using specific techniques, forms, improving performance skills, offering ideas for content)?
  - perform original work for the new writers? (You can ask for copies of poems beforehand, but be open-minded; they are the artist, after all.)
  - deliver workshops? (Poets will have a more powerful impact on smaller groups, though they may be able to work with larger groups.)

Where finances make this impossible, a facilitator or teacher is more than capable of reproducing this effect – but you need to do it strategically. Start by changing the design of the room. Move any desks away and create a circle with the chairs, or have everyone on the floor, or take everyone outside. Sit amongst the new poets, and talk to them face-to-face, rather than front-of-the-room, standing up. Do all the writing activities and brainstorms with them. Share some of your personal experiences and poetry. Speak to them as experts on their own lives, and therefore, their own words.

Choose poems that stoke the fire

Writing and reading go hand in hand. If you want your poets to write because they want to, not just because it's required, get them reading, watching and listening. If you want them experimenting with language, form, style, movement and voice, prescribe poetry.

Finding ways to get your group connecting to poems and poets is priority number one. Expose them to a variety of model poems (see below) – in every session and every workshop if you can. YouTube is your best friend. Choose poems that your group will connect with, that will suit their age, interests, backgrounds, gender, common experiences and artistic familiarity. Content matters more than form – at least initially. Remember: *people connect with ideas*. As education professor Gerald Reyes put it in a 2006 article:

> It is these connections that allow young poets to be able to feel like they have good ideas too; that their ideas are similar to someone who has a poem printed in a book. It allows them to find a literary mentor. These connections invite young poets to know that they are not alone.

This means you will need to get to know them. Who are the people in your group? What are their interests? What music do they like? What are they reading? What are they going through and what language are they using? Armed with that, you can choose poems that speak to them.

STRIKING A CHORD

One of the best workshops I did with a high school group started with a reading of Hieu Minh Nguyen's poem 'Tater Tot Hot-Dish' (see link, Appendix 1). The poem describes how the poet's family gradually assimilated into American culture and lost their Vietnamese heritage. My students, mainly second-generation Chinese kids, connected immediately with the subject. They knew what it meant to live between two cultures.

We talked about what foods their families eat, whether they were more traditionally Australian or whether their traditions were drawn from another country, and how they felt about that. I asked them how they managed their parents' expectations to uphold their cultural heritage with their own desire to 'fit in'.

They brainstormed about food and other aspects of their cultures; then I said, 'Write a poem.' There was not a stationary pen in the room.

NARCISA

What's a good model poem?

The ideal model poem is spoken or written in the language the new poets already use. Shift your focus from what you wish your group read, to what they actually read. Or watch. Or listen to. Their feedback is essential. If they are responding to something, give more of that until you've really got them hooked, and then you can branch out.

If you're teaching poetry as part of a high school English class, moving away from the classical literary canon and giving value and attention to texts from the 21st century might sound scary. How will you make sure your students have had an experience of these important texts? But a more relevant question is: how can you expect any group that is new to poetry to connect with 'classic' poems before they have developed an appreciation of the form? Introduce your group to spoken word poems through YouTube. Classical works – anything from Shakespearean sonnets to poems by 20th-century modernists like TS Eliot – can be introduced after your group is more comfortable with poetry.

So how do you know if you're onto a good example poem? Ask yourself these questions:

- **Subject**: Is the poem's subject relevant for the specific group you've got? (For example, youth experiences, contemporary issues, issues specific to particular cultural backgrounds.)
- **Language**: Is it spoken or written in the language they know and speak?

- **Tone:** Is it passionate? Is it funny?
- **Feeling:** Do you think it will move your community of writers – intellectually or emotionally?
- **Purpose:** Does it model a specific technique or form? Will it prompt the kind of writing you want the new poets to do?

Some of my favourite spoken word poems to use as models are:

Luka Lesson, 'Amber Lights'

I love this one because it resonates with my own experiences, and with those of many of my students, as it explores the feeling of being in-between: between child and adult, between two or more cultures as the child of migrants or refugees, between belonging and being made to feel like an outsider. It would be great for modelling a range of techniques, but I like it for teaching metaphor and symbolism, as well as for writing poems in a narrative style.

Sarah Kay, 'A Love Letter from the Toothbrush to the Bicycle Tyre'

A great one if you're teaching personification. Sarah Kay plays with this technique in a fun way, yet comments on human relationships. I've never met a group that didn't like this poem. One teacher I know showed their group a written copy and only revealed the title after some discussion – the kids' minds were blown!

Pages Matam, Elizabeth Acevedo and George Yamazawa, 'Unforgettable'

'Unforgettable' is a powerhouse performance by three poets, each from a different cultural background, coming together to speak about the importance of names to cultural identity. It is an excellent model for group performance.

Helen Latukefu, 'Pejwok'

This poem was performed for The Rumble Youth Slam in 2018 (now called the Australian Poetry Slam Youth). The poet is a great role model for young writers, and her poem could be used to demonstrate the use of literary devices like imagery, metaphor, apostrophes and many more.

Candy Royalle, 'Stained'

'Stained' takes a hard and confronting look at the difference between nationalism and a love of one's country. Candy Royalle is a magnetic performer.

Sonya Renee Taylor, 'My Mother's Belly'

A personal favourite. This poem is a great example of a poet who has dug into her heart and shared something deeply personal – a reflection on her mother's importance to her in both her life and death. It's a wonderful model for using concrete and figurative language and much more.

APPRECIATING DIFFERENCE

To inspire a group of Year 10 students to explore and appreciate the ways in which they are different from others, I played them a series of poems (see links, Appendix 1):

- **Kevin Jin, 'Why do you have it?'**: The young Australian poet/comedian celebrates his rat's tail in recognition of its symbolic significance to him, and in defiance of social judgment.

- **Steven Oliver, 'Real'**: Oliver is an Aboriginal writer and actor; in this poem he criticises the tendency of non-Aboriginal people to question his Aboriginality.

- **Neil Hilborn, 'OCD'**: In this dynamic poem (mentioned earlier as a great starter poem for groups), Hilborn reveals what it's like to experience life and relationships with obsessive-compulsive disorder.

The everyday language and humour in these poems connects with their audiences. My students *got* them, and this got them thinking about, and ultimately writing about, their own 'otherness'.

I then asked them to make a list of ways in which they are different from others: What makes you different? Unique? What do you have that others don't? What sets you apart from your friends? What makes you different from your family? What about at school? Think about how you're different from the society in which we live. What experiences have you had that are unique? Can you think of a time when someone made you *feel* different, even though you're not? When you felt left out? Cast out? Like you don't belong?

I gave them lots of time to think and remember, to write and make lists. Then they wrote a poem.

NARCISA

Samuel Getachew, 'Flight'

A poignant poem by a young poet, exploring the importance of his heritage to his identity and sense of belonging.

Taylor Mali, 'Totally like whatever, you know?'

Taylor Mali is known for being a commanding speaker, and that's what this poem is about – speaking with conviction. A great model for using tone of voice, modulation, inflection, enunciation, pause and emphasis in the performance of a poem.

Where to find your poems

Videos are obviously a great way to bring poems to life, and there are countless great poems and performances to be found online. I find it helps to provide a copy of the printed text alongside the video for your group to keep, and briefly annotate if you wish.

If you can, have a collection of books of poetry by modern poets you can share with your group. If you're working in a school, you could ask the librarian to buy some. Songs are also a great starting point for reluctant groups. (See Chapter 9 for some more great written or 'page' poems to use as models.)

If you are writing too, share that work with your group, but do this as a model poem at the start or at the end of a workshop, so as not to encourage a sense of competition with you (it can be very daunting to follow the teacher or mentor's example!). Even if you think your poetry is not amazing, it can be helpful to normalise poetry as a part of life. After all, you will be providing them with lots of other examples of writing anyway.

Build a sense of community

For most young people, sharing a piece of themselves, either in writing or aloud with their peers, is downright scary. The same is true for most adults. But there is something we can do to transform this fear into excitement: create a sense of community among the members of your group.

In a spoken word program, all participants – especially young people – should be made to feel like they belong to this group and that it is a safe space for true self-expression and vulnerability. They will share their work as long as they feel confident that the room is free of judgment and that they will not be embarrassed.

Where possible, in a school context I recommend not censoring student compositions for language or content. Allowing them to write as their authentic selves will make their engagement deeper and lasting. It will mean that they will come to each session ready and willing. Establish a group consensus on what is okay. For example, as a group you may decide to allow swearing as long as the swear words are chosen for effect in the context of the work. However, you will likely agree that sexist, racist, homophobic or otherwise offensive material is not allowed.

Sensitive experiences and topics will inevitably pop up, and in a classroom or community situation, facilitators must follow required reporting duties and/or refer

SHARING A POEM

When introducing the topic of 'Language, Identity and Culture' to a Year 12 group, I opened with a performance of a piece I had recently written about my mother baking Bosnian pastries. Here are its final lines:

> She would sift and knead
>> her lips pursed in the effort
>> But she knew the pita would not be the
>>> same
>> that we would be stretched and moulded
>>> into unfamiliar shapes
>> holograms of the crop she planted back
>>> home
>
>> Yet she baked, the glow of the oven
> keeping her warm

I asked students to form pairs and choose one or two lines that spoke to them or stood out. It soon became obvious that the experience of a migrant parent trying to instil their native culture in their children was familiar to my students – being ushered to church every week, continually reminded to speak in their native tongue, persuaded to join a traditional dance group. It was easy, then, to segue into talking about how culture shapes identity, and how the language used in the poem expresses this complex relationship.

NARCISA

TEACH THIS — AFFIRMATIONS

Try a variation on this exercise that I once participated in, during a workshop run by African–American poet Mahogany L Browne. She got us to think of something that we really needed to hear at this point in our lives. Then we paired up, put our hands on each other's shoulders and waited for her cue to say it to each other, one pair at a time. Phrases like, 'You are enough', 'Everything will be okay', 'I love you', and 'Just be yourself' echoed through the room.

participants to a counsellor or a relevant community group for help. However, a sense of community and support is paramount. Everyone in the room should feel like family.

Ten ideas to establish a sense of family

The most important thing is to make a steady, consistent effort to cement the supportive environment – in every session, every workshop, every interaction. It's not enough to just choose two or three of the strategies below; you need to commit to them, all the way, at every opportunity. A wonderful way to make sure this happens is to allow yourself to get attached. If this group, and this program, is part of your life's blood, and if you take those opportunities to be vulnerable with the group as well, then this will really be something.

Idea 1: Break the ice

Give time to icebreaker activities to build enthusiasm for the workshop as well as make writers feel comfortable with one another. These will initially cut into writing time, but they will help your budding poets know that they're in it together. Choose activities that your group will find fun, and be super enthusiastic about them: your enthusiasm is contagious.

For one of my advanced-level English classes, I adapted an activity from Jen Weiss and Scott Herndon's book *Brave New Voices*. I started by asking students to write a description, or a series of words and/or phrases, to describe someone or something in the school (like a subject, a place, a teacher) without using its name. When each student read theirs out loud, the others had to guess what/who was being described. This icebreaker had them in stitches, especially when some students decided to add character voices and gestures.

Idea 2: Roll with the punches

If something isn't working or you have dead air, refocus and re-energise the group with a fun icebreaker. In one session I was working with a group on a narrative-style poem activity, but I soon realised they weren't connecting with it at all. Instead of carrying on with it, I admitted it

TEACH THIS — ICEBREAKERS

- Ask writers to say their name and the title of the movie about their life.
- Ask writers to say their name and an animal that represents them (and why).
- Ask writers to say their name and their favourite toy when they were little.
- Try drama games like 'Yes, let's!' Standing in a circle, one person performs an action, at the same time saying what they're doing – 'I'm hugging a lion!' The next person copies the action and introduces a new one – 'Yes, and I'm taking the lion for a walk!' – and so on until everyone has had a go.
- Ask writers to create a desert island wish list (one person, one food, one object).
- Play a word association game – you start with a word, like 'cloud', the next person says the first word that pops into their head, and so on.
- Play the board game 'Taboo'. In teams, writers must describe a word to their team without using several taboo words typically used for it. If your word was 'soccer', taboo words might be 'sport', 'ball' and 'kick'). You can buy board games based on words, like Taboo or Articulate, in most toy or game shops.

Find more suggestions for icebreaker games on pages 198–201.

TEACH THIS

HELPING RELUCTANT SHARERS

These activities can help a group feel more comfortable sharing their work.

- Divide the group into smaller groups and give each one a different poem. Each group prepares a performance of the poem, using voice, gesture and movement. Of course, if they have written their own work as a group, this can be performed too! Alternatively, if you are working on performance skills, they can perform the same poem but with a different tone, speed and so on. This takes some of the pressure off as they are not performing their own work yet and they are not alone.

- Distribute a copy of a longer poem. Go around the circle, with each poet reading one line. You can also use this strategy to teach vocal modulation: tell them to read in different vocal tones, volumes and pitches so they can see the impact of these techniques.

- Break the group into pairs and take them outside. Position the two members of each pair in front of each other, and give each of them a few lines of a poem (their own or someone else's). They speak their lines to each other, then take two steps back and repeat. They take four steps back and repeat. They take six steps back – you get the picture. The idea is to create a great distance between them so the quieter poets are forced to project their voices. You can then have them move closer again, but challenge them to keep up the same volume.

wasn't really hitting the mark, so I got them to stand up, switch seats with someone on the other side of the room and play two rounds of word association. A few minutes is all it took to get them back in, and then I hopped onto YouTube and chose another poem that I knew would win them over again.

Idea 3: Ease into sharing

Encourage and praise sharing, but don't force it if a member of your group is particularly shy. The easiest and quickest way to make it okay for anyone to share is to keep it short and sweet. With a quiet group, try making it a rule that everyone has to share something, even if it's only one line, two words, or as much as they want. No big deal, no fuss – just get up, speak for 2 seconds and it's done. You should find that they'll gradually share more and more as the sessions progress. Using small sharing circles also helps.

Idea 4: Make some noise!

Click, clap, cheer – make some noise for the poet on the stage! Encourage your poets to click their fingers when another poet is sharing something that resonates with them. Alternatively, one poet can count down 3-2-1 at the end of a performance or reading, and the entire group can give one community clap of hands in recognition. Waiting for applause can make the atmosphere competitive, or at the very least make poets wary of the judgment of their listeners. Clicks or a single clap make sure they feel recognised and valued without fear of embarrassment.

Idea 5: Use cohesive language

Refer to group members as 'poets' and the group as 'family' at every opportunity. Language has a lot to do with how we define ourselves and how we see ourselves fitting in. Simply by using the words, you are telling your poets 'You belong here' and 'We are with you'. It doesn't hurt to actually say that to them, too.

Idea 6: Respect the mic

Teach writers to 'respect the mic' – whoever is speaking/reading/performing has the floor (whether you are using a real microphone or not!). Some groups might have more challenging behaviour. In these situations, it helps to have a professional poet or teaching artist with you at the start. When I was teaching a chatty group, I repeated the phrase 'Respect the mic' at every chance I had, clicking my fingers right before saying it. Eventually I only needed to click to remind them, and even that dropped off as they learned to not only respect each other but be genuinely interested in hearing each other's work. You might want to have a stand-in 'mic', like a highlighter or talking pen, to reinforce the message. If you have transformed a corner of the room into a stage, why not use a real mic too?

Idea 7: Have a mantra

Repeat a mantra at the start and/or end (e.g. 'When I say "We are ...", you say "family". When I say "This is my ...", you say "living room"'). I saw this in action at a workshop run by the non-profit spoken word organisation

Young Chicago Authors. The facilitator loudly and confidently called out the refrain and everyone chimed in. The buy-in automatically increased as the audience became more attentive, respectful and open. YCA has had a key role in transforming the lives of young people and artists in Chicago, chiefly by cultivating an inclusive artist community.

Idea 8: Be upbeat

Be enthusiastic, show your excitement and give approval to anything produced early on. Stay positive, saving your suggestions for improvement for later – perhaps one-on-one – until the group has gained confidence and you can begin modelling feedback. When one of my students produced a shout-out poem about spaghetti, I made him believe I loved it. It takes a lot of energy, especially in the early days, to be upbeat and enthusiastic about everything you hear, but that energy will be returned to you tenfold.

Idea 9: Use collaborative writing and performance

Pair, small-group and whole-group poems bring your reluctant and shy poets into the spotlight and boost their confidence. They know they are not alone and have the support of their team. They also get the opportunity to absorb each other's ideas, language and creativity.

You could start by showing them some examples of group poems. Melbourne's OutLoud youth poetry program, a fast-growing competition where teams of students write, choreograph and perform their original work, shares plenty of these on YouTube (search

WORKING TOGETHER

'[The spoken word] unit focused so much more on how can we bring out the best in each other and how can we listen harder to each other's stories ... I think that it has made for a better classroom culture. I think it can affect the way kids learn together in the next stage of learning.'

Penny Horsley, English teacher

'OutLoud Australia'), and there are many others from the nation-wide US competitions Louder Than a Bomb and Brave New Voices.

Fun, bite-sized experiences of whole-group or whole-class poem writing can also break the ice (see suggestions, pages 117 and 120). Give them a broad topic. I've seen a group of four girls write a poem about women's rights, each girl writing about a different part of the body as a metaphor for a greater issue. A group of five boys each told a story of chasing after a girl who said she wasn't interested, with the piece culminating in a message for all men as they spoke partly in unison. You can encourage movement and gesture to give the poem more theatricality. (See pages 117–20 for some more on group writing and performing.)

Idea 10: Show that you care

Show your support for your group members as people. The biggest takeaway here is to listen. *Really* listen. Listen to what the poets are telling you about their lives; what they want to write about; and what they want to read, hear and see. Show genuine concern about them. Only when they feel that you care about them, and that the group cares about them, will they feel truly comfortable to dig in.

So far, we've looked at the key initial steps you need to take to set the right kind of environment for your spoken word community. You've learned how to set up a writing community, whether that is a club, a community group or an in-school program. You've reached out to poets and spent hours reading and watching poems that you hope will engage your new poets and inspire their own poetry. You've decided on how you will use the strategies to build a sense of community. You're bubbling over with excitement and almost ready! In the next chapter, we look at five ideas to help answer the question: how do you get them writing, editing and performing?

9

AWAKEN THE ARTIST WITHIN

The next step is teaching your spoken word group the skills for writing and performance: how to read and watch poetry, how to write and rewrite, and how to set the stage for performance. But remember that you're not just teaching your novice poets to appreciate poetry, to write it or to share it with others. You're teaching them to *love* it. Poetry will enrich their lives. They will discover quickly that they are full of stories, and that those stories are worth telling. What's more, telling these stories will help them feel something amazing.

Get them reading poetry

Reading and viewing poems is one of the most important steps to learning to write and perform them. You can introduce a variety of texts: page poetry (i.e. poems written for the page, not primarily for performance), song lyrics, music videos, news clips, short stories … anything goes. (If you're following the workshop structure outlined on pages 196–97, this would be step 2, 'Model the writing'.)

> # THEIR WRITING, THEIR RULES
>
> 'We just create the space, we build the stage, and we get out of the way. We let our kids do with that space whatever they want.'
>
> Simon Kindt, English teacher and poet

Here are some of my favourite page poems to use in a spoken word program. Some of these poems would have originally been performed on a stage, but a video version may not be currently available. A list of texts and where to find them can be found in Appendix 1.

Warsan Shire, 'Home'
If I need to make a huge impact and/or tap into emotions, this is the poem I go to. 'Home' confronts negative pre-conceptions about refugees and shocks us by depicting the horrors they have faced.

José Olivarez, 'Home Court'
Another haunting poem, this time about grief. A powerful way to demonstrate imagery and concrete language, or as an example of how to write about place.

Ali Cobby Eckermann, 'Black Deaths in Custody'

A compact poem about the inequalities in the Australian justice system, with some terse, confronting images. It would serve to demonstrate that sometimes 'less is more', or to invite poets to write about injustices they are aware of.

Samuel Wagan Watson, 'White Stucco Dreaming'

Since so many of the poems I choose tend to be serious and dark, I like to break things up by looking at a more joyful poem like this. Watson reflects on the happy memories of his childhood with some playful imagery. The poem also touches on a more serious social issue, but could still be used to prompt writing about memories.

Natasha Trethewey, 'Providence'

'Providence' is about the aftermath of a devastating storm. It can provoke interesting discussion about how to use space, pause and enjambment or how to choose words wisely for impact.

Ask, don't tell

You can provide a paper copy of a poem and unpack any unfamiliar language or necessary background knowledge (though keep this simple) … but what then?

You will probably read the model poem you've chosen ahead of time and reflect on what you want your group to understand about it, but here's where a spoken word program differs from others: you need to know when

SPEAK LESS, ASK MORE

I got some insight into helping young people find their own answers when I was helping my seven-year-old nephew write a speech for school. I asked him questions about his experiences and what he thought others might learn if he shared them. Over and over, I heard him say 'I don't know', watched him turn to his mother for answers, and try to distract me with a funny remark so I might forget the question.

Instead of letting it slide, I pressed on. I soon found that if I rephrased the question, gave an example, made it seem like I needed his help to come up with a word and – most importantly – waited long enough, an independent answer was waiting for me. It wasn't that he didn't know; it was that he was afraid to be 'wrong'.

The same can be said of young people everywhere. Given the opportunity, the right attitude and *time*, they have so much more to offer. When they have the space to find their own answers, they learn to trust in themselves and risk having a go. This applies to reading and interpreting poems, as well as writing them.

NARCISA

not to speak. Instead of driving the conversation about a poem, gently draw your writers in by asking *them* to find points of connection. It's all about asking the right questions and leaving enough space for them to figure it out for themselves. Your questions should aim to find the bridge between the poem and the personal experiences in your group. Jon Sands, a New York teaching artist, encourages his students to connect the poems they read or watch to their own lives, stating: 'I am not the ambassador of what is the truth of this poem.'

Your group members, not you, are the authority on the truth of a poem. Encourage them to find an entry point into each poem; a line, an image, a rhythm, a sound, an experience they've had. This sends them on a quest to find other points of connection, and ultimately leads them to explore the whole poem. After all, how a poet intended their poem to be interpreted is rarely the point – at least for our purposes here. How a poet's words connect with the heart and mind of the reader is paramount. Questions of what the author intended, especially in a school context, can come in time.

Question carefully

So, try to avoid questions like these at the beginning of a spoken word program:

- What is the poem about?
- What are the themes of the poem?
- What was this poet's purpose?

Instead, start with questions like:

- What do you notice about the poem?
- Are there any things the poet is describing that you've experienced too?
- What did you connect with in the poem?
- Circle, underline or highlight what you find interesting in the poem or what stands out.
- Identify all the times the poet uses [a particular word, sound devices, sensory imagery, personification, use of jargon or slang, words that relate to the extended metaphor, words that create a particular tone, etc.]. This can even be a group task.

Then ask the group what they annotated. Ask other group members if they annotated that part too, or something else. When you have built a little confidence, you can start asking why, but this will come voluntarily as they gain experience and as you validate what they say. Remember, the poem is for them, not for you.

Whatever questions you ask, make sure they are not high-stakes questions that can create a deer-in-the-headlights situation. Try not to dissect or annotate the poem in extreme detail either. A few key points is all you need to demonstrate the reason why you are looking at *this* model. Then move on. After all, this is a *writing* (or performing) workshop.

As poets become more confident and engaged, deeper discussions of purpose and meaning should occur.

THE CONVERSATION IS A DANCE

'The class discussion ... it is a dance ... a living organism. You don't want to push the conversation, but it still has to be deliberate. I come up with brainstorm lists (prompts) from the poem we're looking at and, whilst I might have a theory of where I want the discussion to go or what the poem is about, I try to balance my input with agency from the kids.'

Jon Sands, teaching artist

Guide the discussion

Keep in mind that new poets also need your voice – just not so much that it drowns out theirs. The dialogue will be driven by them, but it still needs a *little* steering. You might, for example, give your group a little background information about the poet, the poem, when it was written and so on, which will direct the conversation a little. You might ask them to look at a particular phrase and consider why the poet chose these particular words. You might give them a little help – suggesting that the poem is about a relationship, for example – and then ask them to work out what kind of relationship – is it romantic, familial, friendship, loving, estranged?

Using **Warsan Shire's 'Home'** as a model poem (see link, Appendix 1), a group discussion might go something like this:

Facilitator: Now we've read the poem a few times and I asked you to find something that jumps out at you and make a note on the page. What did you pick?

Participant 1: I highlighted the first bit, 'no one leaves home unless / home is the mouth of a shark'.

Facilitator: 'Home is the mouth of a shark.' What made you pick that?

Participant 1: It's just an interesting way to talk about your home, as if your home is a scary place. I liked how she said that … you can picture a really bad situation.

Facilitator: It does sound like a bad situation. Does anyone think they might know what kind of situation it could be?

Participant 2: I think she's talking about refugees and how there might be a war or something in their country, so they have to leave.

Facilitator: They have to leave?

Participant 2: Yeah, like they have no choice. Like she's saying: why would anyone leave their home unless they had to? Because they weren't safe there.

Facilitator: Who agrees with that?

[**Participants** raise hands, nod.]

Facilitator: It's like she wanted to use this metaphor of home being a shark's mouth to say something to the people who think that refugees are just out for better

EXPECT THE UNEXPECTED

Chicago teaching artist Robbie Q Telfer describes a moment that affirmed for him how much young people have to offer.

'One of my favourite moments was a workshop about what poetry sometimes is – trying to turn ugly things into usable things. That's what a poet tries to do. I used Naomi Shihab Nye's poem 'Valentine for Ernest Mann' as a model for making something ugly beautiful. I asked the kids to make a list of ten ugly things and then write a poem to make one of those ugly things beautiful. This one girl raised her hand and said, "I have racism on my list. How you do make racism beautiful?"

'I asked the class. One boy raised his hand and said, "It's not that racism is good, but it brings people together to fight it, and those communities are what's beautiful." This was a group of seventh-graders. Trusting that the students have a lot to offer in each class is a big part of it.'

opportunities. What does she want to tell them, those who judge the refugees?

Participant 3: They don't want to leave their home, where they belong. This long section here that goes 'the / go home blacks / refugees / dirty immigrants …', this bit about 'they smell strange / savage' – it's all the racist stuff people say to refugees. Even she uses the n-word, and I thought – whoa.

Facilitator: I wonder why she puts that in there. Can you read that stanza out for us again?

[**Participant 3** reads.]

Participant 4: She's using the insults to show how badly refugees are treated, but she's saying it doesn't matter. The bit 'the insults are easier / to swallow / than rubble / than bone' … it's better to suffer racism than to have your family die in your home country.

Ultimately, you will learn when to speak and when to step back. Stay open-minded too; your group may see something in the poem you didn't expect.

OWNING THE LANGUAGE

'If we're teaching kids what poetry is and what language is, the best way to do that is to make them feel like it's theirs. They will want to understand what a noun and a verb is if they're trying to find the right verb to express what they feel about their lives.'

Penny Horsley, English teacher

Get them writing in workshops

In a writing workshop, your goal should be to have your group writing within the first 15 minutes. Free writing is essential. Brainstorming is your power tool, and scaffolding can be used too, when needed. If you see your group a few times a week, have them write one or two poems each week.

If your writers aren't already lovers of language, it's a good idea to focus your initial workshops on ideas, rather than form or technique. Let them know they can just put their words on the page, and not worry about writing techniques (at first). Give them inspiring, accessible model poems and prompts for writing that are focused on their experiences, the people in their lives, their beliefs and so on. Once they're starting to adopt the identity of a writer, you can look at writing techniques and poetic form.

What do we write about?

All people are experts on their own lives, and that is really the only tool they need to get started. Listen to your writers' voices and encourage them to express their experiences. Encourage them to incorporate their own language and anything else that suits them, whether that be movement, percussion, music, even another language.

To tap into all this life experience, start a conversation. While the group is talking and sharing, you may want to write some of their ideas up on a board in bullet

NO RULES

If you have group members with a hearing impairment, learning difficulty or writing impediment, they don't have to play by the rules. There aren't any! They can get someone else to write what they say, they can use pictures instead of words, they can prepare a rough plan and perform, they can perform in Auslan or signed English – they can pretty much do anything! Taking the focus away from spelling and grammar helps too.

points or just ask them to make notes in their journals. Don't forget about all the model poems – they can be used as a launch pad in a session, inspiring writers with ideas, techniques and form.

Workshop ideas

Idea 1: Free writing

The purest form of free writing is just setting the clock for 5–10 minutes and setting pen to paper. No distractions. No instructions. (See Miles's 'vomit onto the page' technique, pages 24–27.) But some groups may need a little more help to get started. These free writing ideas should help clear writer's block and encourage creative flow. Free writing can work well as a regular feature at the beginning of writing sessions.

Tell your writers they will be free writing for *x* number of minutes. The rules? No pausing, no overthinking, no editing, no spelling or grammar checks. This isn't poetry, or storytelling, or anything with a particular shape or form. It's just words on a page, flowing like water. Choose from one of these ideas or develop your own!

- Open a dictionary and choose 4–6 words at random, choosing a mixture of nouns, verbs, adjectives, adverbs, etc. Write one or two on the board. The poets write as fast as they can, without stopping, but must incorporate each of the words at your instruction – you add the words one at a time.
- Play an instrumental piece of music as background. Try a variety of styles and moods.
- Play a meditation track from YouTube as background (e.g. rain falling, a running stream, waves, rainforest sounds).
- Project an image of an interesting place (a city, an abandoned place, a natural wonder).
- Project an image of an everyday object (a window, a lock, a photograph, a leaf, a light bulb, a mobile phone, a letter, a box, a tree, a piece of luggage, keys).
- Bring in a newspaper or magazine and give each poet a different page – go!
- Bring a bunch of images of places, people, objects, artworks (anything!) and scatter them throughout the room. Each poet chooses one to write from.
- Go outside. Sit on a bench, under a tree, in the grass.

Close your eyes or look around. Write what you see, feel, hear, smell.

- Sometimes the first few words are the hardest – try these:
    - How did I get here?
    - There was a sound.
    - Every bone in my body tells me …
    - The cat said, 'Woof.'
    - Blue.
    - Do they even know?
    - The door …
    - Her/his hands/eyes/cheeks/shoulders …
    - This was it. This was the moment …
    - My pen is travelling at a million miles a second.

When the time runs out, you can move on to the workshop you've prepared, or you can ask your poets to use what they've written to start a new poem. Grab a highlighter and select single words, phrases or sentences from their passages, and use those as starting points.

Idea 2: When everything changed

This workshop idea builds on two of Miles's writing ideas from Chapter 2: 'Six senses' (pages 32–35) and 'Your turning points' (pages 44–47).

Ask writers to think about a time or a moment in their lives when something changed. Give them a few moments to think and write. Then add in some further questions, slooowly, to prompt more thinking and writing:

1   Think of some different times in your life when something changed.
2   Maybe it was something that changed your mind, opened your eyes, transformed your attitudes or beliefs or point of view?
3   Has something ever happened that changed your life? Did you ever lose something or someone?
4   Did you find or discover something? Meet someone? Go somewhere?
5   Think of something in your life you would like to change – a dream, a wish.

Give them a few minutes to think and brainstorm. Then open a discussion. Once they have some ideas in their journals – and you might have some ideas on the board too – give some more prompts:

1   From your list of ideas, choose one specific change. Circle it.
2   Picture that moment of change. If you could go back in time and take a photo of that moment, what would the photo look like? What would you see?
3   If you could imagine the moment like a scene in a movie, what would you hear? What sounds, if any? What words, if any, were spoken?
4   What physical sensations do you remember feeling?
5   What smells do you remember? What tastes?
6   Do you remember movement?
7   What about how you felt inside?

8 Was anyone there or were you alone? What were they like?

9 What did you want to happen? What did you want to do?

... and so on.

At this point, their journals should be populated with notes – words, phrases, images. Now you need to inspire a little. Tell them that the memory, the story they are thinking of – is unique and it needs to be told. It wants to find expression on the page. It wants to be heard. Now ask them to break out of the circle and write a poem about their change.

Idea 3: Thinking of you

This workshop develops the idea of using concrete language and building a picture of action (see Chapter 2, 'Write a picture of action', pages 27–32.) Depending on the prompts you use and how your group writes, it can also teach characters and voice.

Play and read aloud **Luka Lesson's 'Yiayia (Grandmother)'** (see link, Appendix 1). Ask writers some simple questions to generate a discussion about the poem ('digging in to the poem'), such as:

- What did you notice about the poem?
- Who was the poem about? Do you feel warmly or coldly towards that person? How do you think the poet feels about them? What words does the poet use to show his feelings?

- What words or phrases or images jumped out at you? Make a note of them. (You may want to play the video again to give an opportunity for a deeper experience of it.)
- Can you picture the person being described? Where in the poem does the poet help us picture her? Which words?

Now turn the conversation to the broader topic of people in our lives who we love and appreciate. Start by asking about the group's grandparents and parents – what are (or were) they like? What do they do with their time? When do you see them? How do they speak, walk and so on? Next, ask them if there is another person in their lives who they love and appreciate, someone important who contributes a lot to their lives.

Next, play and read aloud **Sonya Renee Taylor's 'My Mother's Belly'** (see link, Appendix 1). This poem is a brilliant and moving piece that is perfect for demonstrating authenticity and vulnerability (see Chapter 2, 'Authenticity and vulnerability', pages 66–72).

Dig into the poem with some questions. For example:
- What did you notice about the poem?
- Who was the poem about? How does the poet feel about that person? What words does the poet use to show her feelings?
- What words or phrases or images stood out for you? Share them. (You may want to play the video again.)

Next, prompt writers through a brainstorm and into a writing prompt, taking lots of time to pause and add extra ideas, making sure every writer is able to think of something:

1   Picture the person you love and appreciate and write down their name.
2   Now picture them doing an action you've seen them do over and over, something typical, routine, everyday. Write it down.
3   Describe the action – their posture, their hands, their face, their eyes while they are doing it, and so on. Your description can just be a list of words or phrases.
4   Now think of a specific memory with them – something you did together or somewhere you went. Maybe it was something you did together many times, maybe just once. Write down the memory.
5   Describe the place: the location, the season, the weather, the air, the scent, the people around you and so on.
6   Describe the action: the movement, the person's face, how you felt and so on.
7   Now think about their past: what major things have happened to them? What have they been through? What amazing things have they done? Think about their struggles; their hopes, dreams and ambitions; their achievements. If you don't know, find out! Go home and research, ask someone who might know, or ask them directly, then come back to this page.

8   Now think about the future – if this person wasn't around anymore for some reason, how would you feel? Write that down. Now think about what parts of them you could keep with you if they were gone. They can be actual objects that represent the person, or could be personality traits, abilities or skills.

9   Now, using some of the details you've written down, and any others you think of, write a poem about the person. You might choose to write in present tense to give it a sense of immediacy.

I'm always amazed at the profound poetry that is born when young poets write about the people in their lives. Hai Xia Wang-Pole's poem – its title translates to 'Mum' – gave her an opportunity to reconcile differences between her own childhood and her mother's, and to appreciate the sacrifices her mother made for their family. The poem was inspired by writing workshops at her school.

妈妈

My back aches
Mum weaves baskets with deft fingers
She carries pigs' food 40 kilometres
Malnourished strength
I tell her my shoulders hurt
She carries this family
I carry them far away
Games of balance
Like the paths of rice fields

We catch fishes and frogs with slippery fingers
Dropping fireworks into small rivers
Green like the mud that splatters up the side of
   our clay home
Sweaty fingers
These nails break
Western influence
I am but a diluted version of her strength
So,
I pick up the same rocks
Wear the same old shoes
Tug at this basket
And try, for once
To appreciate

Idea 4: In protest

This workshop, depending on which poem is chosen, can develop a number of writing techniques. See the specific poems listed for ideas.

Ask your writers to brainstorm and then share:

- times when you have been told to do something you didn't want to do
- things you have been being forced to do, or participate in, or believe
- ways in which society has pushed you to conform to a certain standard, to be a certain way, to believe something, etc.

- times when your own mind has stopped you from doing what you want or getting what you need
- things you do not like: Seasons, time of the day or night, days of the week, types of people, experiences (loneliness, racism, doubt, love, prejudice), problems in society, annoying habits, environmental issues, etc.
- times when you have resisted or rebelled against people's expectations or demands – or times when you have wanted to
- times when you have stood up for something, or wanted to stand up for something or someone.

Choose one or more of the poems below (see links, Appendix 1), or find others that explore the idea of resistance:

- **Maya Angelou's 'Still I Rise'** could develop your writers' awareness of the power of metaphor and refrain. With a rhythm and rhyme structure, it also builds on Miles's 'Rhythm, metre, rhyme' ideas on pages 57–66. I also love discussing voice and tone with this one.
- **Suheir Hammad's 'What I Will'** is a powerful protest against war and may need that little bit of context before viewing. It can shine a spotlight on extended metaphor and rhythm.

- **Amit Majmudar's 'Dothead'** tells a story of a moment of change when staring into the face of prejudice.
- **Daniel Beaty's 'Run Black Man Run'** is another commanding performance (see also page 191). You could use it to give an example of characters and voice, as the poem is a conversation between himself and the self-doubt that plagues him.
- **Luka Lesson's 'Please Resist Me'** is wonderful for teaching rhythm, rhyme and metre as well as other sound techniques like alliteration and assonance, as it talks about how challenges in life build strength and bring about change.

Play and/or read the poem you choose. Dig into the poem with some simple questions (like the ones on pages 254–55), dotting in some context where needed.

Ask your poets to write – as an act of defiance or protest – a poem that responds to something they don't like. They can also write a battle poem or a poem that is written as a letter to a person, group or idea.

This can be a really powerful springboard for young poets to address the difficulties they are facing. Morgan Larkin's poem, 'Soldiers', on the next page, helped her tap into feelings of helplessness and made her feel empowered.

Soldiers

Seventeen years gone, we are told **we have
    reached the best year of our lives**.
But unfortunately, this is only the beginning of
    the end
Like this year is Friday,
Everyone knows it's Saturday we're really
    waiting for, yet still we say,
        Thank God it's Friday.

The most important lesson they think they
    taught us is to **always be ourselves**
Except, better.
By now I have a whole jar of eraser dust on my
    bedside table
Scars on my skin like lashings,
Graves of lines of HB pencil
We are the broken matches
Negotiating a kerosene tightrope that just
    won't catch
        With rope around our necks

We are the adults
        Treated like children
            Expected to be adults

**We bear the greatest expectations on our
    shoulders** and

Shoulder-to-shoulder, back to front we stand
in a
Brick-walled box, even though some of us are
Circles or
Triangular-based pyramids,
Every brick is a piece of our personality we're
not 'entitled' to yet;
In the mad rush we all got stuck in the hoop
we're jumping through
Now we're gnawing each other's heads off in
hysteria, making sure we're not
Last.

We are here by **choice**.
We chose this instead of **uncertainty**.
We chose this instead of ridicule by our
parents, and our families.
We chose this like we had a choice.
Humans are a vengeful race, each generation
taking it out on the one below like
That's some kind of justice and
It never ends.

We are taught, that **there is no limit to new
ideas**.
Like
The number of colours isn't limited
and
The alphabet isn't
exhaustive

SLAM YOUR POETRY

Every year the hoop gets higher,
Built upon the shoes of graduates passed
It gets exponentially harder
                    There is no final destination
Every year we move forward
          ***There is someone to take our
               place.***

We are the ultimate ant army.
We are the unwilling soldiers
I am the perfect rectangular prism for their
    boxes
I am conformity
          I am exhausted.

Tears don't do any good anymore because **I**
    can't open my eyes
Lashes holding hands like the shoelaces we
    are told to tie up
Like shirts we are told to
          TUCK IN
and
          TOP BUTTONS
we are told
               TO BE DONE UP
          ***I don't make it from my desk
               to my bed anymore***.

We have been taught to wire our brains
    and our guts together to make a perfectly
    functioning GPS, and that
        Our hearts make for
        misleading guides.

We rebels **hide ourselves**.
We quietly draw maps in eraser dust and set
    them on fire and
Melt our glass hearts into compasses.
We are performance seals jumping through
    hoops
We are trapeze artists and tightrope walkers,
Weaving safety nets from our own veins
Take solace in only each other's words.
        We let our voices hang in the
        air like smoke.

We are seventeen.

Morgan says:

I remember feeling incredibly trapped at that time
of my life – seventeen years old. It felt like I wasn't
an adult but I definitely wasn't a child; I wanted to
do well at school and uni and life, yet I felt I didn't
really own my pathway or my choices. I was angry
at 'the system' of high school, and how stressed it

made me feel. I didn't want to make decisions about the rest of my life at seventeen; yet I felt, at the time, like I had to in order to be successful. This poem was a small way I felt I could rebel, or at least, reach out to the students who would come after me, and let my family (who were a big, supportive part of my education) know how I was feeling and what was going on inside my head and high school. Writing this made me feel like I could reclaim some of my power and make decisions that were entirely my own.

Idea 5: My place / Your place

Ask your writers to brainstorm and discuss:

- places where you feel or have felt out of place, uncomfortable, unhappy, unsafe or as if you didn't belong
- times when you had to go/stay/move somewhere you didn't want to or didn't like
- places where you feel or have felt at home, comfortable and happy; if you're upset or unhappy, where do you go?
- your favourite spots to hang out in your home, your neighbourhood, your city, your country or the world.

Now ask them to look over their list of places and think about the memories associated with them. Which one has a strong memory? Or, which one is really important to you? Which one makes your blood boil or turn cold? Which has a huge effect on you?

Next, ask them to think about *why*. With the places that have negative memories, why are they negative? What made you so uncomfortable, unhappy or unsafe? And the places where you were happy? What was the reason? Get them to write it down.

Then encourage writers to think about place in another way. Thinking of the places where you feel at home, are there people who don't feel at home there? Why? And the places you don't belong, who does belong there? Why?

Now ask them to pick one place and circle it.

Read and/or play one or more of the poems below (see links, Appendix 1), or another of your choice that focuses on place:

- **Omar Musa's 'Capital Letters'** captures the essence of the suburbs, using them as a springboard to talk about disadvantage and self-empowerment. This poem could help crystallise concrete language, the six senses and authenticity.
- **José Olivarez's 'Home Court'** (mentioned on page 227).
- **Sarah Kay's 'Montauk'** uses a narrative style and clear imagery to depict the joy of a special place and its role in her growing up. Just be aware, there's the odd swear word in this one here and there.

If needed, before your group writes their 'place' poem, you can scaffold their writing with some further brainstorming on the place they have chosen from their list:

- List the people who are typically at this place.
- Write the words, phrases and sentences you would typically hear there.
- What things do you there? Describe the action/ movement.
- List the smells and tastes and other sounds of this place.
- What can you see there?

Now ask your poets to write a poem about the place or describe a scene there. Encourage them to experiment with one or more of the techniques used by the model poets – narrative writing, sensory imagery, concrete and figurative language or anything you draw out from the poems.

Idea 6: Building metaphors

Start with a brief explanation of what a metaphor is (see Chapter 2, pages 40–44.)

Read and/or listen to **Warsan Shire's 'Home'** (see page 294), or any other poem with a metaphor, then dig into the poem with a few simple questions:

- What jumps out at you?
- Which lines are really powerful?

- Can you find all the metaphors in the poem? Why is the poet comparing these two things?

Draw up a table on the board and ask your writers to call out random places to fill one side. Then ask them to call out the name of an experience, a feeling, a person or an object to fill the other side. For example, you might have:

A place	An experience, feeling, person or object
The bottom of the ocean	Love
A cliff edge	My father
Home	A knife
The kitchen	Losing your phone

Now ask writers to work with a partner or two within the group and look for similarities between the things in the first column and those in the second. Can they find a way in which a cliff edge is love? Can the bottom of the ocean be your father? Can home be a knife? Then discuss as a group how some of these comparisons can actually be true.

Draw their attention to the fact that what they're doing is using metaphors. Now ask them to pick one, or come up with a new one, and write a stanza to describe it. You can then either ask them to build this into a complete poem, or to create a fun team activity. They could form a group with other poets who chose the same place and work on their individual stanzas together to create a poem.

You can mix it up a little too. Instead of 'place' being in the first column, try an action, an animal, a sound, a taste or even a smell. Experiment with it! This is exactly what Chloe Willett did for her poem 'Nympherior', written at school in a writing workshop with a visiting poet. She says, 'This poem [was] developed in a workshop with Bill Moran on our own monsters. The methodology involved demonstrated to me that I do not need to wait for inspiration – I can create it.'

Nympherior

Nympherior is on the stage of every ceremony.
Her liquid wax remoulding your fingerprint so
    it is not you grasping the award, but her.
She sends her plastic trophies to roar from the
    lights above you.
You cannot feel when her wax solidifies over
    you and you are sent with bruised coins to
    scuttle into sidewalk cracks.
You cannot see her except for when she has
    already encapsulated the no-longer-you.
The mirror is the only sign of her presence,
    aside from the muted glow from the wax
    sealing your pores and lips.
You can only then see her crystal cataracts
    glow and fade, reflecting a dull prediction of
    your future.
A ritual to dispel her is to stand in the sun until
    she whimpers at your feet.

Scrub your fingertips so only you remain.
Exfoliate your skin under scalding water;
    remind yourself that you did not give her
    permission.
This feeling is only outside of you, outside of
    your skin.
Don't be better than others, for you will
    become her.
Better yourself.

Idea 7: Extending metaphors

This workshop should help your writers learn how to write using extended metaphor.

Ask writers to brainstorm a long list of words associated with a place, season, object, event or time, such as:

- a garden
- the ocean or water
- a storm
- a window or door
- a house
- winter.

Share some answers as a group and write them up on the board. For example, for ocean/water you might have something like:

pools	wave	blue	foam	deep/depth
reflection	cold	swimming	wading	diving
mirror	beach	sand	shells	horizon
drops	clean	wash	pebbles	rocks

Repeat the activity with at least one or two more words.

Now ask them to look at each group of words and think of people in their lives who share something in common with those places or objects. You might ask: who in your life is like a garden or gardener to you? Are you like a garden or gardener to someone? How? Who is like the ocean? Who is a storm? Ask them to write down *how* these people have done this. What have they done? What qualities do they have?

Prompt your writers to write a poem about one person in their lives who is like one of the places or objects listed. They should use the word bank they have developed to make the metaphor clear and perhaps even transform it into an extended metaphor.

You can change this workshop up by having them reflect on a time or event in their lives that was like a storm, a winter, a door and so on. You could also add a model poem to show your group how it works. **Franny Choi's 'Mud'** (see Appendix 1, Text poems), for example, uses a series of extended metaphors to reflect on relationships.

Tahlia McConochie's poem, 'I went too far', written while participating in a spoken word program at her school, shows us how two extended metaphors can work together.

I went too far

Swam out past the rocks
and bled
so you could see how real I was,
how unhesitating.

You wouldn't hold me other than a few times
and I took to you like one would to driftwood
   somewhere in
the middle of the Pacific.
I was desperately
absurdly calm
as inside me began to blaze
as my skin flowered open and red-black,
as I scrambled to find a foothold.

Just when I thought I might know you,
you jumped through a hole in the floorboards
like a small animal unknown to domesticity.
I woke up with the curtains open
the room nearly empty
everything burning white and a low moan
   coming from the centre of my chest.

When I stood
I fell
into the centre of the Pacific
with no months,
no driftwood,
no proof that anything had ever been.

Idea 8: The list poem

This workshop activity includes a great model poem and gives writers the freedom to write about anything they want while giving them a solid structure to work with.

Ask writers to make a few lists:

- things you are grateful for
- difficult times or moments in your life
- things someone has done for you
- things someone has taught you
- things people should know about you
- things you wish you had known
- advice you would give to teenage girls/boys.

Watch and briefly discuss **George Yamazawa's '10 Things You Should Know About Being an Asian from the South'** (see link, Appendix 1).

Prompt poets to write a list poem about one of the topics they brainstormed, or something else.

For more workshop ideas, check out the Young Chicago Authors blog (youngchicagoauthors.org/blog).

But I still don't know what to write!

Open discussions, brainstorms, prompts and scaffolds should be all your writers need to decide what to write.

TEACH THIS

PROMPT QUESTIONS

If a member of your group is struggling with free-writing exercises, try these prompt questions:

- When you went to bed last night, what was on your mind? When you woke up this morning, how did you feel?
- When was the last time you felt a big emotion – when you were angry, sad, truly happy, nostalgic, etc.?
- What's the most important relationship in your life right now?
- What's worrying you these days?
- Think about a problem you've had that you've overcome, or a problem you're still trying to navigate.

But if a new writer still asks you what to write about, or if you are doing a free-writing exercise, instead of providing answers or specific suggestions, *pose questions*. In really tough cases, write a question or two on the board or on a post-it note and leave the writer with it. Try not to hover – give them space. If you see they are still struggling, try opening a dialogue with them about the topic, or encouraging them into a discussion on the topic with another member of the group.

Fuel the writing process with feedback

Giving feedback and empowering poets to revise and edit their writing are essential components of a spoken word program. In their book *Brave New Voices*, Jen Weiss and Scott Herndon use the term 'feeding' to describe the feedback process – think of it as the food that fuels a poem's growth.

Giving feedback and encouraging self-feeding

Sometimes, when a new writer asks us to look over their writing to give them feedback, they are asking for our approval. They want to know if they got it 'right'. As mentioned earlier, we as teachers are not the 'experts'; the authority on what works best in our writers' poems should be *them*. Feedback from others is still hugely valuable (more on that later), but we want writers to be able to critically evaluate their own work. The right types of questions are your go-to strategy:

- What's your favourite part/word/phrase/image?
- Which parts are you not sure about?
- How do you want your audience to feel when they hear your poem? What do you want your audience to know or to think about? Think about if you're getting that across.

Once they have had an opportunity to reflect on their own work, your feedback, especially in the early days, should be extremely positive. Start by only giving positive feedback. Make writers feel like champions for almost anything they've written, as long as it comes from an honest place. Praise their work, help them understand why it works, and encourage them to keep doing more of it. Negative comments, even when well-intentioned, can erode self-esteem. However, if you build your relationship with your writers by showing that you care and that you are a warm, accepting and genuinely interested person, they will eventually trust and seek out your opinion.

EFFECTIVE FEEDBACK

'My attention towards negative feedback has really evolved. I found it's not effective at all. It's much more effective to say "Do more of that", to catch them in the act of something good.'

Robbie Q Telfer, teaching artist

Constructive, not negative

When your group is ready for constructive feedback, gradually introduce it by choosing one or two points to focus on. Feedback can and should be provided verbally and in writing. Be specific: choose an image, line or word choice, or focus on the content the writer has chosen to highlight the most interesting or evocative aspect of their poem. In my own experience, highlighting my favourite parts of a poem, explaining their strengths and describing how those parts spoke to me led to more and more of that strength showing up in the writer's work.

Then, as writers gain confidence in their work, slowly build up to more detailed feedback. You can start to suggest ways in which a writer can build on their strengths: by developing a simile into an extended metaphor (see pages 257–60), by directly addressing a person they are writing about, by brainstorming some sensory imagery and so on. Praise them more and more for their efforts, their experimentation, the way they take on feedback, and their drafting and rewriting process; this will build a growth mindset that focuses their attention on development. Eventually, shift the focus of some of your comments away from the specific poem the writer is working on to broader aspects of composition that they can apply across their work.

Feedback from the group

You will also need to coach writers to become each other's 'feeders'. Other group members are your goldmine when it comes to feedback. Model good feedback for the whole group and teach them how to give it explicitly. Tell them they will be responsible for helping improve each other's work and they must pay attention to how to give good feedback. This means when they offer feedback, they say the poet's name and speak to them directly, not to you.

When starting out, or with a quieter or less confident group, it is helpful to give your poets some guidance on what to talk about and how to give feedback.

Questions to ask others, as the poet:

- What did you think my poem was about?
- I wanted to say/show ... Did that come across clearly? How can I make it clearer?
- What mood did you feel when I read it out?
- What were your favourite parts/words/lines/images?
- Did the poem resonate with any of you? (Did you feel like you 'got' it, like it could have easily been about you?)
- Which parts do you think could be strengthened?
- What about the structure of the poem – any suggestions?

TEACH THIS / FEEDING CIRCLES

Empower the poets to give each other feedback through 'feeding circles'. Create small groups and ask them to read out their work within their group for feedback. Insist that the work is read aloud, and that the group members make notes of key images or phrases that stand out.

After a second or third reading, poets can give each other positive feedback and helpful comments that use the best aspects of a poem as a starting place for improvement. Once they have had some time within those groups to get comfortable, you can play musical chairs to mix up any existing friendship groups if needed.

Questions to ask and comments to make if you are giving feedback:

- I like how you have ...
- I liked it when you said ...
- This line is really strong because ...
- This part resonated with me because ...
- I can see how you have ...
- I noticed you chose/used ...

- I think your poem is talking about ...
- I think this part is really clear ... this image could be clearer or stronger ...
- When you said ..., I thought/felt/wondered ...
- A metaphor might be good to show ...
- What if you ...?
- Have you thought about ...?
- In this line, you could ...
- At the end, it might work if you ...

Draft it, then craft it

People often think that great writing just happens – that it's a result of talent. What they don't realise is the hours, days, months and years of toil it actually takes. They need to see it to believe it.

Encourage revision

Here are some suggestions for how you can show your group how important editing and revision are.

- Show the poets a poem at various stages of development, so they can see how much reworking often goes into a finished piece of writing. A quick Google search of 'poem draft edit' should yield some good results. I've shown the original draft of Wilfred Owen's 'Dulce et Decorum Est', along with the published version, to groups so they can see the changes Owen made. It's even better if you've been writing and you can show them your own work in progress.

- Invite writers to give you feedback on something you have written, beginning by asking them quite specific questions. Closed questions like, 'Which word should I choose here: ... or ... ?' and 'Should I start with this line or is this more powerful?' can eventually become open-ended and complex, like 'How can I create a more interesting rhythm?' and 'How can I more clearly represent my point in this stanza?'
- Write a short group poem and then go through the revising process together.
- Leave lots of time for the editing process.

Revision techniques

There are lots of strategies for editing a piece of writing that you can share with your group. Here are just a few.

- In one sentence or a few words, write a summary of the main idea of your poem. Now highlight all the words, phrases and images that build this idea. Cut out the rest and set aside.
- Have a long, hard look at the first stanza or first 5–6 lines. Is this where your poem should really begin? Are the first words engaging? Is a clear and interesting image created immediately? Sometimes you may find you are building up to the real start of the poem, which may be somewhere in the middle.

- Look at each section of your poem and ask yourself if you could say it differently or figuratively. Could you use a metaphor?
- If you used any comparisons (like metaphors, similes, personification, etc.), could you develop them further? Extend them into other lines?
- Look at the line breaks and the ends of the stanzas. These are really important because your readers or listeners will find a pause there, giving those words or images more weight. Can you make them more meaningful or stronger?
- Look at every adjective and adverb you have used. Are they actually needed, or could you have used a more specific noun or verb? Now look at all the verbs – could you be more precise with the verbs you chose?
- Look at all the little words, like *I*, *so*, *the* and so on. Are they needed? Could you create more dramatic impact with fewer words, or focus attention on the important words? (See also Chapter 2, pages 35–40.)
- Look at the beginning and end. Do they fit together? Is there a change or shift by the end? Does the poem come back to the start in some way, like a similar or contrasting image or idea?
- Consider the pacing or speed of the poem. Do you need to use line breaks, punctuation, shorter lines or longer lines to draw attention to specific parts?
- Using the 'Ten ideas to make your writing jump' from Chapter 2 (pages 23–72), ask yourself if there are some ideas you haven't applied. Experiment!

DEVISE, REVISE:
AN EXERCISE

Here is a workshop idea that focuses on revising and editing a piece of writing, and examining and experimenting with word choice.

1   Ask writers if they've ever told the same story of something that happened to them multiple times, to different people. Discuss how when you retell a story, you tell it a different way each time, and often will improve the story – make it more funny, more shocking, more entertaining. Explain that this is why revising a piece of work is so important. You want – you *need* – to do your story justice.

2   Ask writers to write a few sentences, lines or phrases on a given topic or using a line starter, such as:

       Outside my window ...

       My mother ...

       I remember ...

       Noodles ...

       The things I keep ...

       The best feeling ...

3   Hand out slips of paper. Ask writers to choose one line from their list and copy it onto the paper.

4   Writers then pass their slip to the next person/ another writer. If the group is still quite reserved about their work, you can ask them to put all their slips in the middle or in a hat and then choose one, so no one knows who wrote what.

5   Ask writers to read the lines to themselves and consider them carefully. They are allowed to make one change – they can add a word or piece of punctuation, take away a word, change a word or change the order of words.
Repeat steps 4 and 5 a few more times.

6   Divide writers into small teams. Ask them to write a poem together, combining the lines of writing they have to create a new piece of work. They can simply organise the lines in a sequence, without any editing, or you can challenge them to make some edits along the way.

7   Each team shares their poem with the whole group.

8   Finish with a discussion of how revising the lines, and piecing the different parts together, affected the final product. Ask them if they think any of the poems could be further revised and how.

9   Now have writers take out a poem they've written recently and revise it. Less experienced writers can be encouraged to first highlight their favourite parts of the poem (a single word, a phrase, the overall topic, a line, a stanza, etc.) and to develop those parts by either writing a new poem around them or elaborating on those elements. You can also pair writers up and have them help each other identify the strongest parts.

- Read the poem out loud, again and again. This is by far the best editing tool there is! Trust your gut feeling about whether it's right or it needs changing. An even better strategy is to read it to someone else.

See more editing ideas (editing tools) on pages 200 and 201.

Using feedback to revise

As highlighted earlier ('Feedback from the group', pages 265–67), group feedback is great for helping writers find out if their poem has clarity, and if it's having the effect they want. Get them to reflect on the feedback they've received, then have them rewrite (and rewrite and rewrite) the poem. New versions of a poem should be shared again with the same people to 'test out' the poem and show the other writers how helpful their feedback has been.

Take it from page to stage

The live performance to a writing community is what breathing is to living. Once your writers have had opportunities to write, rewrite and share their writing in an informal way, it's time to put them in the spotlight.

In preparation for a live performance with an audience, provide opportunities for your writers to experiment with different ways to perform their poetry. You want them to experiment with:

- their voices – accent, stress, volume, pace, tone, rhythm, pause, emotional quality or tone, any noises they can make with their mouths
- their bodies – facial expressions, movement, posture, hand/arm gestures, creating accents on particular words through gesture, syncopating particular words or images with gestures and gaze, making percussion.

Give them time to workshop this in small groups and try things out many times. Poems should be rehearsed multiple times – alone and in front of an audience of supportive peers and/or family, who can give constructive feedback. It's fun to go a little crazy, but when it comes time to make decisions, encourage them to keep it natural. (See Miles's 'Sample workshop exercises for performing writing', page 135, for some ideas.)

As Sarah Temporal explains, spoken word poetry is not the same as acting. Unless a part of your poem actually embodies another person's voice, performing a poem is not about becoming somebody else. If your poem is about a moment in your life, bring yourself back into that moment, embody the emotions you felt, be vulnerable and be real.

Performing a poem can help a writer see how to perform it better next time. How the audience reacts, how the words feel across their lips, how their body moves in tandem with the words – all these things should help them find what feels 'right'.

USING THE BODY

'With performance, just keep in mind you're not training [performing writers] to do unnatural things with their body. You want to recognise the tools they already have and show them different ways of using them. One example is having them read a poem three different ways. Watch them rehearse and give feedback on specific good moments ... Workshop with them how to have presence, to be in the moment.'

Jon Sands, teaching artist

Have your writers annotate their poem with performance instructions. For example, highlight the words you will stress; draw a red cross where you will pause; use arrows to indicate where you will increase your pace, volume or pitch; add notes on movement, gesture, and so on. A great idea would be to show them this technique in action – distribute a poem that you have annotated and then perform it. Ask them for suggestions for changes and experiment with effects.

Put on a show

The first time I asked my Year 9 students to perform their work in a mini-showcase, I felt a sprinkling of fairy dust in the air. They were going to perform one poem in front of 29 of their peers. Suddenly, everything they wrote *mattered*. It is common knowledge that having an authentic audience for your work is important, but an audience of your peers and a live performance? This was something even better. They got that all-powerful intrinsic motivation to write and revise a quality piece of work. New changes were made, gestures were added, voices got that little bit louder.

An authentic performance event, with an MC, a mic, a real stage, a real audience and some glittering lights will not only motivate your budding poets to read, write, revise and rehearse, but will also give them a huge confidence boost. Having a real audience is crucial. Teacher and poet Troy Wong recalls his students' reactions after a performance: 'There's a buzz they have. There's a glow when they've come off stage ... That kind of experience, I never got that in high school ... so there's a real value in that.'

So how do you put on a show?

The school slam

If you're running a slam for adults, have a look at Miles's chapters 4, 5 and 6 in this book. He covers what a slam is, setting up the event and running it on the day, and has included some useful documents as appendixes (pages 296–331) to help you.

Here, I'll focus on running a slam for a school, a setting that has its own specific requirements. Poetry slams can have a powerful effect on young people, especially at school. They can be organised at lunchtimes, after school or on a special night. Here are some tips for setting up a school slam.

Plan early

- Go and see a live poetry slam. This will give you an idea of how it works.
- Get some support. This is a major event and you will need the backing of the school executive, so show them why running a slam would be great for the students and the school.
- Book a location: the school library or hall, or even a small local theatre.
- Talk to the head of your music or creative/dramatic arts department, who is likely to have lots of experience in running events. Ask what sound/ lighting equipment the school has, where it's stored, who can help you set it up, and if there are any students who already know how to run the equipment.

Enlist help

- Next, enlist the help of your student representative groups for help with:

- making and putting up promotional posters
- making a promotional video to show at a school assembly
- being ushers for the night
- setting up and packing up chairs for the performers and the audience.
- Find a **sacrificial poet** – a teacher or student who is not competing – to perform a poem just before the slam begins to test out the audience judges.
- Book in a **feature poet or performer** – a poet, singer, guitarist, ensemble; anything goes! – to entertain the crowd while the scores are tallied.
- You will also need helpers to do the following jobs on the day:
  - **sound/lighting:** at least two experienced students to run the equipment and play music as each poet takes the stage; make sure they get there an hour early to set up and are clear on what they have to do
  - **timekeeper:** a person to time the performers
  - **scorekeeper:** a person to record and tally scores for each performer
  - **camera person:** a person to take photos and/or record video
  - **extra helpers:** one or two extras on-hand at the event to do any jobs you can't do yourself – unexpected things always pop up
  - **MC:** optional. You can MC, or you can ask an entertaining public speaker like a student or teacher at the school

- **teachers**: to help out with crowd control, if needed
- **school caretaker or librarian**: to make sure the space is available, unlocked and ready for the slam to be set up, and to advise on locking up.

Promote and prepare

- Source your equipment. See pages 152–54 for the equipment you'll need.
- Promote the event. Have one of your poets do a sneak preview at a school assembly, show a video promo and/or have your poets visit classrooms to perform a piece.
- Set up a Facebook event and, if the slam is open to the public, have all your poets promote the event on their Instagram, Twitter or other social media feeds, if your school policies allow it. Email parents if you have the facility to do so.
- Prepare your performers. Since a slam is a competitive event, your poets will need to volunteer to compete. If you think you might struggle to get enough poets, try doing a team slam: form groups of 2–4 poets and get them to prepare team poems. Poems should be 2–3 minutes long, but they can be longer if they are team poems.
- Have your poets prepare at least two poems in case of a tie.
- Once you have a list of competing poets, write them all down on slips of paper and pop them into a box

or hat. Running order will be random. Make sure they have all arrived before you start!

- Make a program. A simple program will look something like this:

1 MC welcome
2 Five audience judges selected (e.g. MC throws five lollies into the crowd)
3 The rules (MC explains how the slam works, the rules for performers, how the judges will score, how the winner is chosen, prizes)
4 Sacrificial poet
5 The slam (poets perform, judges score)
6 Feature poet or performer
7 Results and prizes (second runner-up, first runner-up, champion).

On the day

Bring on the day:

- the poets' names to throw into a hat
- copies of the program for you, the helpers and performers
- one clipboard for you, for your program
- five clipboards, five black markers and plenty of paper for the judges to display their scores
- a scoring sheet, pen and clipboard for the scorekeeper
- extra pens
- prizes

- several mics – the MC will keep one, plus an extra for the performer; you will need more if doing team poems
- lollies to throw into the crowd to select the five audience judges
- jug of water and glasses for yourself, other helpers and performers – position these with easy access during the show.

The open mic

Another event option for any spoken word group is a regular open mic (see pages 124–26), which can happen almost anywhere and anytime – in a classroom, school hall, café, local library, community space and so on. Open mics are non-competitive, and the poems performed don't have to be perfect. Far from it! They are often read from scrunched-up pieces of paper or a smartphone.

Some tips for organising an open mic:

- Depending on the poets' age and confidence, decide to either nominate who will perform in advance, or have poets 'sign up' on the day.
- Choose a location. A classroom can be used if you're working with a school group; if your poets are over 18, a pub on a weeknight is another great option. Local library and community spaces also work well.
- Create or find a stage. Even in a basic space you can make one with borrowed materials – some black wooden platforms, a black curtain hung behind

performers, a spotlight (a lantern, lamp or an actual spotlight) and a microphone hooked up to an amp. A music stand can be supplied for holding the poem text, freeing up poets to use their hands.

- Assign a confident group member to be the MC and show them some videos of MCs to prepare them. Alternatively, you take on the role or ask a friend.
- Consider asking one of your group members to play some music before the show, and/or before each performer while the audience applauds.
- Teach your group to be vocal. Open mics and slams are LOUD, so encourage your group to click, clap, cheer, stomp their feet – show their love for the poets!

The showcase

Finally, the showcase is the perfect platform for showing off the growth of each individual poet and allowing them to share in a celebration of poetry. Unlike a slam, there is no competition or judgment, only the feelgood vibes from an appreciative audience. Showcases tend to be organised as part of a spoken word program, at a venue such as a hall, a library or a small theatre.

Showcases are a fantastic alternative to slams, as they take off some of the competitive heat that would otherwise create a few nervous wrecks. Younger writers and groups that are particularly anxious or shy benefit from this kind of non-competitive environment.

Some tips for putting on a showcase:

- Let your poets know about the showcase from the beginning of their program, and advertise it.
- Involve the poets in the organisation of the event.
- Experiment with a variety of performance types, including pair and group poems, theatre and audience involvement.
- Invite everybody – students, parents, community, local schools, you name it!
- Prepare the poets by giving lots of time for preparation, rehearsals and performance skill workshops. You can even stage a mini showcase like a dress rehearsal.
- Find an experienced public speaker to be your MC. The MC is hugely important to build the right atmosphere at a showcase, rallying the audience to cheer for the poets and building a supportive, energetic mood.
- Seek helping hands to help with set-up and pack-up.
- If you can, get a DJ (maybe someone in the group) to play some energetic music at the start, the end and as poets are walking on stage. You can also use music during the interval if you have one.
- If you're struggling to get interest up or organisation done, team up with another event, like a writer's festival, a library or council event, or a school music night.
- Invite a professional poet or two to be a 'feature' for the event.

Multimedia and beyond

Live performance isn't the only way to get your poets' work out into the spotlight. Create a group YouTube channel. Get your poets to film themselves and create spoken word videos or even music videos; just make sure you've got parental permission covered where needed. SoundCloud is another option for uploading audio content.

Other options include publishing a chapbook (a book of works written by the poets); publishing/printing poems and displaying them around a school, library or community arts centre; or creating an immersive 'walk-through' theatre experience. The sky's the limit.

SOURCES AND REFERENCES

Poems and extracts

Extracts and full poems are from the following sources, with permission where required:

Samuel Taylor Coleridge, 'Kubla Khan', 1816, www.
    poetryfoundation.org/poems/43991/kubla-khan
TS Eliot, 'The Love Song of J. Alfred Prufrock',
    1915, www.poetryfoundation.org/poetrymagazine/
    poems/44212/the-love-song-of-j-alfred-prufrock
Jesus Govea IV, 'Bleeding into Grass', supplied by Jesus
    Govea, 2019
Hannah Green, 'Note to Dancers', 2016, published in
    the anthology *Spoken Word Club Chapbook 2015–
    2016*, Chicago: Oak Park and River Forest High
    School, 2016
Zohab Zee Khan, 'He Said', published in 'Four poems
    – Zohab Khan', *Critical Muslim*, 2019, www.
    criticalmuslim.io/four-poems-4/
Morgan Larkin, 'Soldiers', supplied by Morgan Larkin,
    2019

Tahlia McConochie, 'He, with no more pressing matter to pursue' and 'I went too far', supplied by Tahlia McConochie, 2019

Megan McMahon, '5 Cent Coin', supplied by Megan McMahon, 2019

Jesse Oliver, 'Dream Revolution', 2017, www.youtube.com/watch?v=btcOkowu5_g

Hai Xia Wang-Pole, '妈妈', published in the anthology *the sky of us, alight*, Brisbane: Kelvin Grove State College, 2015

Phil Wilcox, 'This Microphone Only Tells the Truth', 2015, www.youtube.com/watch?v=TRnnyGKGAkE

Chloe Willett, 'Nympherior', supplied by Chloe Willett, 2019

Interviews

Quotes from writers, poets and teachers are taken from the following sources, with permission:

Brianna, student: Interview with Narcisa Nozica, 3 July 2018

Maxine Beneba Clarke: Interview with Miles Merrill, 3 April 2018

Polly Cotton: Interview with Narcisa Nozica, 22 July 2018

Emily Crocker: Interview with Narcisa Nozica, 11 April 2018

Lorin Elizabeth: Sarah Fallon and Lorin Elizabeth, 'It's never enough said with Lorin Elizabeth', Word

Travels, 12 July 2018, www.wordtravels.info/
blog/2018/7/10/uwc4c5y3m1ujjyetntm1zf1o5q7tqx
Hannah Green: Email correspondence with Narcisa
Nozica, 15 August 2018
Tiffany Harris: Email to Miles Merrill, 25 November
2018
Penny Horsley: Interview with Narcisa Nozica, 24 July
2018
Sarah Jane Justice: Email to Miles Merrill, 19 November
2018
Simon Kindt: Interview with Narcisa Nozica, 12 April
2017
Zohab Zee Khan: Interview with Miles Merrill,
24 August 2018
Luka Lesson: Kirsti Whalen and Luka Lesson, 'On point
and powerful: An interview with Luka Lesson', *The
Pantograph Punch*, 19 June 2015, www.pantograph-
punch.com/post/luka-lesson
Omar Musa: Hannah Hall and Omar Musa, 'Hannah
Hall interviews Omar Musa', *Cordite*, 1 February
2017, cordite.org.au/interviews/hall-musa/3/
– Amanda Craig and Omar Musa, 'Enough said about
Omar Musa?', South Coast Writers Centre, 24 April
2017, southcoastwriters.org.au/news/2017/enough-
said-about-omar-musa
Candy Royalle: Sarah Fallon and Candy Royalle,
'An interview with Candy Royalle', Word
Travels, 13 April 2018, www.wordtravels.info/
blog/2018/4/13/candy-royalle

Jon Sands: Interview with Narcisa Nozica, 24 February 2017

Benjamin Solah: From Benjamin Solah, 'On the mic for the first time: 8 tips for your first open mic performance', Melbourne Spoken Word, 2 July 2019, melbournespokenword.com/on-the-mic-for-the-first-time-8-tips-for-your-first-open-mic-performance/

Neil Smith: Email to Miles Merrill, 15 November 2018

Robbie Q Telfer: Interview with Narcisa Nozica, 3 August 2017

Sarah Temporal: Interview with Narcisa Nozica, 12 February 2019

Troy Wong: Interview with Narcisa Nozica, 12 March 2018

References: books, articles

Page 168 Susan Weinstein, 'Kids engage much more ...':

Weinstein, S., cited in Nozica, N. (2017). Spotlight on poetry. *mETAphor*, no. 2, 2017, p. 25.

Page 174 A new sense of self:

Reyes, G.T. (2006). Finding the poetic high: Building a spoken word poetry community and culture of creative, caring, and critical intellectuals. *Multicultural Education*, vol. 14, no. 2, pp. 10–15.

Weinstein, S. & West, A. (2012). Call and responsibility: Critical questions for youth spoken word poetry.

Harvard Educational Review, vol. 82, no. 2, pp. 282–302.

Page 179 Spoken word programs improve school attendance, retention, academic performance and understanding of artistic craft:

Fisher, M.T. (2003). Open mics and open minds: Spoken word poetry in African Diaspora Participatory Literacy Communities. *Harvard Educational Review*, vol. 73, no. 3, pp. 362–389.

Fisher, M.T. (2005). From the coffee house to the school house: The promise and potential of spoken word poetry in school contexts. *English Education*, vol. 37, no. 2, pp. 115–131.

Fisher, M.T. (2007). *Writing in Rhythm: Spoken word poetry in urban classrooms.* New York: Teachers College Press.

Jocson, K. (2005). Taking it to the mic: Pedagogy of June Jordan's Poetry for the People and partnership with an urban high school. *English Education*, vol. 37, no. 2, pp. 132–148.

Jocson, K. (2006). There's a better word: Urban youth rewriting their social worlds through poetry. *Journal of Adolescent & Adult Literacy*, vol. 49, no. 8, pp. 700–707.

Jocson, K. (2008). *Youth Poets: Empowering literacies in and out of schools.* New York: Peter Lang.

Rabkin, N., Reynolds, M., Hedberg, E. & Shelby, J. (2011). *Teaching Artists and the Future of Education: A report on the Teaching Artist Research Project.*

Chicago: NORC at the University of Chicago, www. norc.org/pdfs/tarp%20findings/teaching_artists_ research_project_final_report_%209-14-11.pdf

Reyes, G.T. (2006). [*as above*]

Weinstein, S. (2010). 'A Unified Poet Alliance': The personal and social outcomes of youth spoken word poetry programming. *International Journal of Education and the Arts*, vol. 11, no. 2, files.eric. ed.gov/fulltext/EJ881569.pdf

Page 185 Spoken word for all levels of writing and reading ability:

Reyes, G.T. (2006). [*as above*]

Page 189 The English curriculum:

ACARA (n.d.). *English: The Australian curriculum.* www.australiancurriculum.edu.au/f-10-curriculum/ english/

Page 207 Gerald Reyes, 'It is these connections that allow …':

Reyes, G.T. (2006). [*as above*]

Page 262 'In their book Brave New Voices …':

Weiss, J. & Herndon, S. (2001). *Brave New Voices: The Youth Speaks guide to teaching spoken-word poetry.* Portsmouth, NH: Heinemann.

Page 273 Sarah Temporal: spoken word poetry is not the same as acting:

Temporal, S. (2018). SlamCraft: Tell the truth [blog post], 8 September, sarahtemporal.com/2018/09/08/slamcraft-tell-the-truth/

Further reading

Eleveld, M. (ed.) (2003). *The Spoken Word Revolution: (slam, hip-hop & the poetry of a new generation)*. Naperville, IL: Sourcebooks MediaFusion.

Eleveld, M. (2007). *The Spoken Word Revolution Redux*. Naperville, IL: Sourcebooks MediaFusion.

Jocson, K. (2008). *Youth Poets: Empowering literacies in and out of schools*. New York: Peter Lang.

Raphael, S. (2018). *Limelight*. Melbourne: Puffin Books.

Sitomer, A. & Cirelli, M. (2004). *Hip-Hop Poetry and the Classics*. Los Angeles: Milk Mug Publishing.

Smith, M. & Kraynak, J. *Stage a Poetry Slam: Creating performance poetry events*. Naperville, IL: Sourcebooks MediaFusion, 2009.

Weinstein, S. (2018). *The Room Is on Fire: The history, pedagogy, and practice of youth spoken word poetry*. Albany, NY: SUNY Press.

Weiss, J. & Herndon, S. (2001). *Brave New Voices: The Youth Speaks guide to teaching spoken-word poetry*. Portsmouth, NH: Heinemann.

APPENDIX 1
POEMS AND RESOURCES ONLINE

These lists are just a sample of great poems and online resources for writing, performing and teaching spoken word poetry. All the poems mentioned in the book are listed here, plus some other favourites, but there are many, many more to be found!

Spoken word poems and readings

Maya Angelou, 'Still I Rise'
    www.youtube.com/watch?v=qviM_GnJbOM
Daniel Beaty, 'Knock Knock'
    www.youtube.com/watch?v=9eYH0AFx6yI
Daniel Beaty, 'Run Black Man Run'
    www.youtube.com/watch?v=QAB9zD8Q6MQ
Candy Bowers, 'Australia, I love you. But …'
    www.youtube.com/watch?v=yYwOS1mHnfA
Arielle Cottingham, 'Tramlines'
    www.youtube.com/watch?v=yocCysa0wPg
Sage Francis, 'The Best of Times'
    www.youtube.com/watch?v=VA8hzUDXvtk

Samuel Getachew, 'Flight'
www.youtube.com/watch?v=8cPKHMZAgU8
Suheir Hammad, 'What I Will'
www.youtube.com/watch?v=LFbE8RBhSDw
Neil Hilborn, 'OCD' www.youtube.com/
watch?v=vnKZ4pdSU-s
Kevin Jin, 'Why do you have it?'
www.youtube.com/watch?v=FZ57angmCGM
Marshall Davis Jones, 'Spelling Father'
vimeo.com/67922579
Sarah Kay, 'A Love Letter from the
Toothbrush to the Bicycle Tyre'
www.youtube.com/watch?v=BIAQENsqcuM
Sarah Kay, 'Montauk'
www.youtube.com/watch?v=qdLmHCwciCY
Shane Koyczan, 'To This Day'
www.youtube.com/watch?v=ltun92DfnPY
Shane Koyczan, 'We are More'
www.youtube.com/watch?v=Hqe-I3a7ZPk
Helen Latukefu, 'Pejwok'
www.youtube.com/watch?v=yJAvrbmjw9Y
Luka Lesson, 'Amber Lights'
www.youtube.com/watch?v=iBE1vmYSSZk
Luka Lesson, 'Please Resist Me'
www.youtube.com/watch?v=D-HED2Uxwbw
Luka Lesson, 'Yiayia (Grandmother)'
www.youtube.com/watch?v=D-HED2UXwbw
Amit Majmudar, 'Dothead'
www.youtube.com/watch?v=RJm49gtVvaE

Pages Matam, Elizabeth Acevedo & George
Yamazawa, 'Unforgettable' www.youtube.com/
watch?v=Xvah3E1fP20

Taylor Mali, 'Totally like whatever, you know?'
www.youtube.com/watch?v=pKyIw9fs8T4

Miles Merrill, 'Talking with My Daughter about Race'
www.youtube.com/watch?v=yL8BqfyM2XM

Miles Merrill, 'The Flying Triangle' www.youtube.com/
watch?v=44R2RCGIyF8

Tim Minchin, 'Storm' www.youtube.com/
watch?v=HhGuXCuDb1U

Melanie Mununggurr-Williams, 'I Run'
www.youtube.com/watch?v=x03nIylz4Hg

Omar Musa, 'Capital Letters'
www.youtube.com/watch?v=XZfJsOGOxnw

Steven Oliver, 'Real'
www.youtube.com/watch?v=GW3dks0Eu5Q

Candy Royalle, 'Love'
www.youtube.com/watch?v=F4z3FaZw6ro&t=1s

Candy Royalle, 'Stained'
www.youtube.com/watch?v=f2sZYFAYJX4

Mike Taylor, 'Thinking About You'
www.youtube.com/watch?v=P0QiFy8dmX0

Sonya Renee Taylor, 'My Mother's Belly'
www.youtube.com/watch?v=tQcZpy2oSMU

Reggie Watts, 'Out of Control'
www.youtube.com/watch?v=SmUD0vbSUHg

Phil Wilcox, 'Mother's Day OPSM Eyewear'
www.facebook.com/watch/?v=1227894653918117

George Yamazawa, '10 Things You Should Know About
Being an Asian from the South'
www.youtube.com/watch?v=8PkWgMNC_z4

Spoken word video collections

Australian Poetry Slam on YouTube
www.youtube.com/user/AustralianPoetrySlam/videos
Button Poetry on YouTube
www.youtube.com/user/ButtonPoetry/videos
Def Poetry Jam performances on YouTube
www.youtube.com (search 'Def Poetry Jam')
OutLoud! on YouTube
www.youtube.com (search 'OutLoud Australia')
Spoken word for students: YouTube playlists
by Narcisa (Nicole) Nozica
www.youtube.com/watch?v=Eu9MWTjqpSw&list=
PLLBQ3WEyoCS6izUM35cmUyJeOJDMXyt52

Text poems

William Blake, 'Ah! Sun-flower'
www.poetryfoundation.org/poems/43649/ah-sun-
flower
Franny Choi, 'Mud'
pankmagazine.com (search 'Franny Choi four poems')
Billy Collins, 'Introduction to Poetry'
www.poetryfoundation.org/poems/ (search 'Billy
Collins Introduction to poetry')

Emily Dickinson, 'Wild Nights – Wild Nights!'
www.poetryfoundation.org/poems/44087/wild-nights-
wild-nights-269

Ali Cobby Eckermann, 'Black Deaths in Custody'
www.poetryfoundation.org/poetrymagazine/
poems/89016/black-deaths-in-custody

TS Eliot, 'The Love Song of J. Alfred Prufrock'
www.poetryfoundation.org/poetrymagazine/
poems/44212/the-love-song-of-j-alfred-prufrock

Langston Hughes, 'Boogie: 1 A.M.'
www.poetryfoundation.org/poems/150981/boogie-1-
am

Hieu Minh Nguyen, 'Tater Tot Hot-Dish'
www.radiuslit.org/2014/02/27/three-poems-by-hieu-
minh-nguyen/

Oodgeroo Noonuccal, 'Assimilation – No!'
www.poetrylibrary.edu.au/poets/noonuccal-oodgeroo/
poems/assimilation-no-0719019

José Olivarez, 'Home Court'
www.deepcenter.org/deepcenter/wp-content/
uploads/2017/08/home-court-by-jose-olivarez-2.pdf

Wilfred Owen, 'Dulce et Decorum Est'
www.poetryfoundation.org/poems/46560/dulce-et-
decorum-est

Naomi Shihab Nye, 'Valentine for Ernest Mann'
poets.org/poem/valentine-ernest-mann

Warsan Shire, 'Home'
www1.villanova.edu/content/dam/villanova/mission/
mandm_assets/2016workshop/Home.pdf

Dylan Thomas, 'Do Not Go Gentle into
   That Good Night'
   poets.org/poem/do-not-go-gentle-good-night
Natasha Trethewey, 'Providence'
   www.poetryfoundation.org/poems/56292/providence
Samuel Wagan Watson, 'White Stucco Dreaming'
   www.poetryinternational.org/ (search 'Samuel
   Wagan Watson White Stucco Dreaming')

Organisations, events and resources

Australian Poetry
   www.australianpoetry.org
Australian Poetry Slam
   www.australianpoetryslam.com
– champions
   www.australianpoetryslam.com/champions
– Slam page
   www.australianpoetryslam.com/writearevolution
Australian Poetry Slam Youth
   www.australianpoetryslam.com/australian-poetry-
   slam-youth
Australian Society of Authors
   www.asauthors.org
– rates of pay
   www.asauthors.org/findananswer/rates-of-pay
Bankstown Poetry Slam
   www.bankstownpoetryslam.com/home
Brave New Voices (USA)
   youthspeaks.org/bravenewvoices

Louder than a Bomb (USA)
youngchicagoauthors.org/louder-than-a-bomb
Melbourne Spoken Word (Vic)
melbournespokenword.com
Melbourne Spoken Word & Poetry Festival
www.mswpf.com.au
The Moth
themoth.org
OutLoud (Vic)
www.australianpoetry.org/primary-school-
workshops/
Queensland Poetry Festival
queenslandpoetryfestival.com
Red Room Company
redroomcompany.org
Sarah Temporal's SlamCraft
sarahtemporal.com/slamcraft/
Slamaladingdong (Vic)
www.slamalamadingdong.com.au
SlammED! (Qld)
queenslandpoetryfestival.com/slammed/
Spoken Word SA (SA)
spokenwordsa.com.au
Unspoken Words (NSW)
unspokenwords.org
Word in Hand (NSW)
wordinhand.com.au
Word Travels
www.wordtravels.info

– Spoken word around Australia
   www.wordtravels.info/spoken-word-around-aus-1
Young Chicago Authors
   youngchicagoauthors.org
– blog (spoken word resources)
   youngchicagoauthors.org/blog

APPENDIX 2
SLAM YOUR POETRY: SAMPLE GUIDELINES

This document, while not exhaustive for all situations and conditions, does provide a step-by-step approach to help make your night a success.

Slam checklist

Before the night, you should assemble the materials you'll need. Here's a checklist you can use. (This assumes your venue will have AV sorted.)

Item	Quantity	Description
Blank A5 or A4 paper or mini-whiteboards	c. 60 sheets	Used by scorekeeper and judges to mark down and display scores, respectively. Bring enough sheets for your judges to have one per two slam contestants (using both sides of the paper), so: 5 judges 10 contestants = 5 sheets of paper per judge = 25 sheets. The scorekeeper will also use paper. Other sheets will be needed for miscellaneous other things (see below). Alternatively: 5 small whiteboards with whiteboard markers and a cloth for each, for the judges.
Markers/textas	5	Used by judges to record scores and display them for the MC and scorekeeper. Should make a nice wide mark that can be seen by the MC from the stage.
Pens	Varies	Your scorekeeper and timekeeper will each need one, and you'll need some for sign-ups sheets and hat slips. If you do paper feedback forms, your audience will need some too.
Clipboards	3–4	One for each organiser person so they can carry running orders, contact sheets, etc.
Slam sign-up sheet	1	This is what your contestants will use to declare their intent to participate, and to provide their email and phone contact details. The sheet should be numbered for the number of contestants you will accept on the night, with a column each for name, email and phone contact.
Slam hat slips	1	You will use these to select names from the hat to determine the order of contestants. Each contestant will write their name on a slip.

Slam Your Poetry: sample guidelines

Item	Quantity	Description
Mailing list	1	This is what your audience will write their email addresses on, if they'd like to hear about future events.
Slam scoring sheet	1	Used to record contestant scores, calculate rankings and identify the winners.
Feedback surveys (optional)	30+	These can be paper forms filled in at intermission and returned afterwards; alternatively, give your audience and participants a link to an online survey.
Timer	1	A stopwatch
Timekeeper	1	A person to monitor and record the time taken by each slam contestant.
Small gifts	5	These are thrown into the audience to select the judges. They can be any small Frisbee-like item, even little chocolates.
Hat or box	1	Hat slips are thrown in here. Used for selecting Slam contestants one by one for the stage.
Misc.	N/A	Scissors for cutting 'hat slips', signage like arrows pointing to the venue or reserved seating, Blu Tack for signage.
Device player, iPod/ phone/ MP3 player, musician or band	1	Music to entertain before the show and during breaks. If you have the ability to organise a live band for your event, go for it!
Recording device (audio or video)	1	Used to record each performance. ONLY use the recorded material for archives/ promotion/publishing if you have a release form signed by the contestants BEFORE the end of the evening.
Prize/s	1–3	Negotiable. This can be a gift certificate/cash or gift equivalent.

On the night

Before the slam

- Make sure you have a **timekeeper** and a **scorekeeper** to assist you. These might be two staff members from the venue/festival/event, or two co-organisers of the slam.
- Have some music playing as people arrive.
- Sign poets up for the slam as people come in.
  - Get both email/phone contact details if possible on the **sign-up sheet**.
  - Have a separate **hat slips** sheet where poets write their name in large, clear letters.
  - Have them sign a **release form** if you are recording.
- Have a **mailing list sign-up sheet** for members of the audience to add their email addresses to.
- Tear or cut up the hat slips sheet. Put all the names in the hat or box.
- Turn the music down.
- Start the recording device, if used.

The slam: introductions

- Introduction by MC/host:
  - Open with an Acknowledgment of Country or engage a local elder to give a Welcome to Country.
  - Open with a poetic introduction.
  - Thank the sponsors and others who've helped with the event.

- Let audience know where the exit and the toilets are.
- You might want to provide a short paraphrased explanation of what a slam is.
- Next, choose your five judges from the audience.
- Explain the scoring.
- Introduce the timekeeper and scorekeeper.
- Start the slam!

Choosing judges

- Chose an assistant from the audience. (You might ask a child. This keeps them occupied during the show.) Give them a stack of paper and the five marker pens.
- Throw the five 'gifts' one at a time into the audience. A person who catches one becomes a judge.
  - In small groups, this may be a case of finding out who is not performing and getting them to judge. If a slam contestant catches a 'gift', they pass it to the person behind them.
  - While the 'gifts' are being tossed, the assistant gives a stack of paper and a marker pen to each new judge.

Scoring

- Explain the scoring to the contestants and the audience:
  - The scoring scale is 0.0 to 10.0. Encourage use of decimal points to avoid a tie.

- For each contestant, the top and bottom scores are dropped and the middle three are counted, arriving at the score for that contestant.
- Contestants lose 1 point for every 30 seconds they go over 2 minutes. So at 2:01 they lose a point, at 2:31 they lose another point, etc.
- At 1:50, the timekeeper can make a small 'ding' noise or raise a hand to let the contestant know they're about to go over time.

'Sacrificial' performance by poet

- To the get the judges warmed up, perform a short piece (under 2 minutes) and have them score you.
- This makes the process more obvious to that wary first slam poet drawn from the hat. It also sets a standard for comparison that the judges can use to rate the contestants.
- Alternatively, you might bring a sacrificial poet – someone you know is good but isn't competing.

The slam

- Get someone from the audience to pick a name from the hat/box and shout it out.
- The poet whose name is called performs.
- Thank the poet and ask the judges for their scores. Call out those scores for your scorekeeper.
- If relevant, ask the timekeeper if you think any points were deducted for going over time.
- Thank the poet again.
- Continue to pick from the hat and repeat the process.

Mid-point break

- If there's a full list of 20 slam poets, have 10 of them perform and have a 15-minute break.
- If there are fewer than 20, have a break at the halfway point. With an uneven number of poets, leave the smaller group for after the break.
- Remember to stop audio/video recording during the break and just put music on.
- Alternatively, if there is an extra person handling your recording, get them to interview poets and punters during the break.
- Perhaps encourage people to buy any merchandise you have during the break.

After the mid-point break

- After the break, turn off the music, turn on the recording device and continue drawing names from the hat/box until all contestants have had their turn.
- When all poets have performed, take another break (5–10 minutes) to tally scores.
- Tally the scores and identify the winners.

Winners and prizes

- After the break, announce winners in this sequence:
  – third place
  – second place
  – first place.
- Give prizes, if available, to each as they are announced.

- Only first and second places go to the next round (if applicable).

Thanks and goodnight

- Thank the audience, contestants, timekeeper, scorekeeper and sponsors.
- Perform a closing piece.
- Say goodnight.
- Turn the recording device off and turn the music on.
- Take photos.
- Encourage people to buy any merchandise you have.
- Collect markers, mailing list sheet, slam poet sign-up sheet and release forms.
- Be sure you have a name, email and contact number for the winners.
- Straighten up the venue.

- That's it!

- Have a good time.

APPENDIX 3
SLAM YOUR POETRY: SAMPLE RUNNING ORDER

Poetry slam: Running order

Date / Venue name and address

Sound-check and prep 3:00–7:30 pm / Event 7:30–10:00 pm

3:00 pm	Word Travels organisers arrive.
5:00 pm	2 Word Travels volunteers for backstage setup and support arrive.
	Volunteer induction + roles.
6:00 pm	2 Word Travels volunteers for merch and door arrive.
	Volunteer induction + roles. Set up at front desk.
6:30 pm	Set up. Sound check: **Band**.
6:45 pm	Sound check: **MC**; **Guest performers 1, 2, 3, 4**
7:15 pm	Doors open. **Band** begins.
7:30 pm	**MC**: acknowledgment, introduction to event
7:40 pm	**MC** introduces **Guest 1**
7:45 pm	**MC** introduces the slam and facilitates judge selection
7:50 pm	**Poetry slam begins (half of the poets)**
8:15 pm	**MC** introduces **Guest 2**

8:20 pm	BREAK
	MC invites people to fill in feedback forms, etc., before announcing break.
	Band plays.
8:40 pm	**MC** introduces **Guest 3**
8:45 pm	**MC** thanks **Guest 3** and welcomes everyone back
	Second half of poetry slam (remaining poets)
9:10 pm	**MC** introduces **Guest 4**
9:15 pm	**MC** announces winner, thank yous + plugs
9:20 pm	Event close. **Band** plays.

APPENDIX 4

SLAM YOUR POETRY: SIGN-UP SHEET AND HAT SLIPS

Slam sign-up sheet

Please write legibly.

No.	Name	Contact details
1		Ph:
		Email:
2		Ph:
		Email:
3		Ph:
		Email:
4		Ph:
		Email:
5		Ph:
		Email:

[Organisers: Add extra rows for the number of contestants you have.]

Slam hat slips

Please write your name in large, clear letters.

1	
2	
3	
4	
5	
6	
7	
8	
9	
10	

[Organisers: Add extra rows for the number of contestants you have.]

APPENDIX 5
SLAM YOUR POETRY: SCORING SHEET

Slam scoring sheet

No.	Name	Score 1	Score 2	Score 3	Score 4	Score 5	After omitting high/low score	Final ranking
1								
2								
3								
4								
5								
6								
7								
8								
9								
10								

ACKNOWLEDGMENTS

Miles

Thanks to my partner Sarah Allely and my daughters Billie and Emerald for their patience as I wrote this most nights between 9 pm and 1 am. Woke up tired many times but pushed through the mornings making the porridge and my coffee.

Huge thanks to the all the poets and peers who gave me their time, over the phone and in person. Also a thanks to Word Travels staff and board for keeping all the bits and pieces of Australian Poetry Slam glued together.

A massive thanks to Narcisa for keeping up with the rollercoaster of lulls and mad flurries of writing, for taking this book on and talking through inspiration and doubt.

Thanks to Elspeth Menzies for your continued encouragement and belief in this project. Narcisa and I owe a huge amount of credit to Emma Driver. She totally drove us to completion in the final drafts of the book. Her deadlines, quick turnaround times and ability to tighten up text is hard to keep up with – thanks for leading us to the finish line!

Narcisa

I want to thank Miles, first and foremost, for inviting me to write this book with him, for his openness to my ideas and for being with me every step of the way.

Thank you to the English Teachers Association for their support of my vision, and the folks at NewSouth, particularly Elspeth and Emma D, for their patience, their diligence and their insight.

I would also like to thank all the teachers, teaching artists and poets who shared their voices and experiences with me. Particular mention goes to Peter Kahn, Kevin Coval, Susan Weinstein and Simon Kindt who not only shared their wisdom but opened the door to their spoken word communities from which I learned so much.

Thank you to my Blakehurst High School family, the English faculty, who embraced this crazy new thing from the get-go, and to Bearnard: this labour of love would not have been possible without you manning the fort and being my sounding board.

INDEX

9 781742 236094